TWELVE PILLARS OF
CORRECTNESS

Twelve Pillars of
Correctness

Tommy Hammer

ISBN: 978-1545359167

CONTENTS

1

CHOICE

"I should have a right to choose."

"Of course you should. And you do. You can choose to be anything you want."

"Maybe I shouldn't phrase it as a 'right.' Call it an 'ability.' What I'm missing are identifiable alternatives. Without having a menu of options that people can relate to, I can't present myself and see myself in a meaningful way. The absence of familiar alternatives has taken away my power of choice."

"How can you say that? There are an infinity of possible alternatives. In simple terms, you can think of the options as forming a continuum on which you're totally free to choose any point."

"A continuum from what to what? There are no words to describe its extremes or its polarity or any of its constituent locations. With nothing to hang onto, nobody can interpret what I'm projecting and respond accordingly."

"I think I see your problem. It comes from your fixation on the ways people lived and defined themselves over a hundred years ago. You want stereotypes. You want to fold yourself into the images and behavior patterns that once contaminated the culture. We're now mercifully liberated from these stereotypes, yet you want to bring them back because—I'm sorry, but it's true—you haven't got the personal resources to stand on your own as a truly unique individual."

"Insult my personal resources if you like, but the need I'm talking about is something general, not limited to me. Let's say that one day I find myself wanting to be a 'girl.' You know, a female with—"

"Please try to avoid sexist language. Legal precedents and common decency oblige us to use the scientific terms, namely born-with-vagina and born-with-penis, in the understanding that these are just transient conditions. There are no such things as 'female' and 'male' as ongoing traits."

"Okay, fine, on the given day I want to feel like a certain kind of person who started as a BV. In the language of the past, which I'm now using, the term 'girl' meant a lot more. It implied youthfulness, which generally implied physical attractiveness, which implied suitability as a sex object."

"Why would you want to categorize yourself like that?"

"I'll try to explain, but first will you confirm that I have a legally and morally supported right to want anything that doesn't impinge on other people. Whether or not they can be fulfilled, all desires are legitimate. True?"

"True enough. Under the prevailing norms and judicial guidelines you can want anything at all, no matter how contemptible."

"So on the day in question I want to be a girl. This means looking, feeling and acting in ways that once were generally associated with girls. But there's vastly more to the choice than picking a point on a continuum. All sorts of variables will be involved in my girlish persona. My chosen girlishness will probably be high on some of these variables and low on others, so that the overall package is unique. But the whole construct will be wrapped around the primordial stereotype of girlhood, sometimes cleaving to it and sometimes playing off of it, leaving me identifiable to myself and to others despite my uniqueness.

"We're talking about what I would like to do, not what I would actually achieve under present conditions. Continuing in this vein, let's introduce another person. Suppose that I meet somebody who strikes me as attractive and who might be interested in knowing and perhaps having sex with a girl. I flaunt my girlish persona in various ways, and this person responds in various ways. He or she—"

"Again, please avoid sexist references. Use the correct 'ze.'

"Okay, ze confronts the stereotypical girlhood that I've projected, then proceeds to refine this image based on the cues I provide in the ensuing interaction. In some respects I seem to be *this* sort of girl, whereas in other ways I strike the given individual as *that* sort of girl. My persona is thereby fleshed out as something unique, but what makes it identifiable—both to ze and to me—is its linkage to a succession of girlish stereotypes. The joint project of actualizing me is an interesting and potentially exciting game, no matter where it ultimately leads. But in today's social context this game can't be played. The loss is more than a game; it's an ability to create and project a serviceable identity. Without recourse to stereotypes, I no longer have an ability to choose and deploy a recognizable self."

"That's the silliest thing I ever heard."

"No, it's not silly. Under traditional conditions, the parties to a new interaction would construct images and expectations of each other based on patterns observed in prior acquaintances. Gradually an extrapolation of these patterns would render the behavior of each new party somewhat understandable and predictable to the other. But not entirely, which would make the process an ongoing source of fun. The inherited patterns—which you've chosen to call stereotypes—were central to human identity and perception in general. They came from, and fed back into, our attempts to organize the world. Today their absence leaves us in an amorphous fog with an infinity of meaningless options."

"Look, the transcendence of stereotypes didn't just happen. It was adopted as an explicit social goal, and its achievement has been one of the key triumphs of the progressive era. Maybe stereotypes were an occasional source of fun and games as you've noted, but they operated much more importantly as a source of constraints and discontent. I'm not even talking about the negative stereotypes that were formed on a random basis for the purpose of defaming certain groups. I'm talking about the ones that were most often referenced in positive or neutral terms, like your 'girl' and 'boy.' These stereotypes existed to encourage if not mandate conformity. They told people how to think and how to behave. Persons who couldn't or wouldn't fit into them were left feeling deviant and isolated and persecuted."

"Stereotypes could indeed be constraining, but more often than not they were supportive. Most people didn't want to create themselves out of whole cloth. You've said I lack the resources for this, and I'm saying my condition has always been the rule rather than the exception. Take for example a BP individual growing up in the past. Early on, he—excuse me, ze—learned that ze was supposed to be a 'boy.' Along with this realization came templates of behavior and appearance and so forth that were associated with boyhood. Conforming to the given templates, in adequate but probably varying degrees, gave zirm a boyish identity and a sense of belonging and most likely a good deal of satisfaction. Without this guidance an average kid couldn't easily have acquired these things on zir own."

"Hold it. A minute ago you were talking about the beauty of choice, but now you're extolling lack of choice. What exactly do you want?"

"What I want is a return to the situation wherein stereotypes were available as scaffolding for behavior and identity, but weren't imposed so rigidly that people couldn't manipulate them to their own ends, the way I would do in fashioning myself as a girl. To illustrate what we've lost, consider the case of transsexuals. The share of the population undergoing gender reassignment surgery was always small, but over the past hundred years it's fallen practically to zero. Why? Because there's no longer anything to be reassigned to. At one time a BV individual might grow up wanting to feel like a boy, so at some point ze would have zir anatomy changed to fit this image. But now nobody knows what a boy is. The social arbiters only tell us that such terms should be avoided and genitalia are irrelevant. So potential transsexuals pass up surgery to spend their days in an intersexual limbo."

"How can you possibly claim that the people in question have been rendered worse off? The BV individual in your example wouldn't undergo surgery to become a 'boy' so much as to escape being a 'girl.' The main driver was usually a push, not a pull. With stereotypes now out of the picture, the push is gone and the given individual—untroubled by external forces—is surely better off than ze would have been, no matter what sexual decisions might follow."

"Okay, you're right, I picked a poor case to illustrate individual benefit. But the example is still useful to address overall impact. The number of gender-dysphoric individuals has never exceeded one or two percent of the population. The elimination of gender stereotypes may have made these persons happier as you say, but at a cost of identity reinforcement for a great many more people. By any sort of aggregate calculus the net change has been negative.

"You may have heard about the so-called 'bathroom wars' of a hundred years ago, in which progressives felt that transsexuals should have bathroom access according to their adopted gender while reactive elements wanted access to remain limited on a BV-versus-BP basis. The former policy would have been a very minor change, certainly not worth fighting about, if transsexuals were in fact the only persons involved. The problem was that this population was never delimited, for ethical and perhaps legal reasons. So open access for transsexuals effectively meant open access for anyone with a passing wish to see how the other half lived, and this was what the courts decreed.

"Superficially it's hard to understand the insistence of progressives in this area given the numbers involved. But transsexuals weren't actually their main concern, as shown by the fact that they later persuaded the courts to move beyond sexual identity and eliminate gender-designated bathrooms altogether. The bathroom wars were just a tactical sally in the progressives' larger campaign against gender. Their opponents hardly seemed to know what they were defending—some got fixated on bathroom rape; some saw the fight as a religious matter; almost none cited the role of gender as a support for reproduction—but the progressives never lost sight of their larger counter-gender mission."

"I'm familiar with the bathroom wars, and you're wrong on every point except one. First, it's an accepted principle of modern social policy that numbers don't matter. This principle holds because any liberating initiative on behalf of even one individual cannot fail to benefit everybody else. A collective benefit must accrue because such an initiative becomes a valuable teaching moment, a step toward universal enlightenment. Second, in the bathroom wars there was always a broad element of support for open access, whether because much of the population was already enlightened or because it wanted to be. And third, there's no basis for your blanket assumption that most people stood to lose from the deconstruction of g★★der. A majority of the population consisted of BV individuals for whom everything about g★★der had always been a burden, a source of 'pain and sorrow.' Such individuals invariably stood to gain from its demise—as a basis of social interaction and as an operative concept—although this lesson sometimes required a sequence of teaching moments to take hold. The one point you've gotten right is that the most critical support for bathroom liberation did indeed involve its role in the campaign against g★★der. This role was entirely appropriate given the overriding importance of that campaign, and the progressives advancing it would have been happy to admit what they were doing if anyone had asked."

"Well, it's obvious that we're never going to agree on very much. I can only take another tack and point out that gender was an irreplaceable part of our reproductive strategy. In its absence the country's indigenous population is rapidly declining. We're on a path of enlightenment that would leave us with just one perfect person."

"So be it. Numbers don't matter."

"Of course, the population won't drop that far because immigrants will take over the country long before then. These immigrants will come from, and cling to, atavistic cultures that allow them to maintain their numbers the old-fashioned way. So what will disappear won't be people per se but the demographically unsustainable package of progressive values that you consider our salvation."

"Enough of your foolishness. The last time we met, I noticed you were kind of cute, which got me thinking that we might want to have sex. With this in mind I've prepared a contract in hopes of gaining your approval. Actually I've got two contracts, specifying different acts and positions depending on whether you're BP or BV, which I don't happen to know."

"I'm BV, thank you very much. Let me see your contract for that case. Hmm... Looks okay. I'll sign, but on one condition. You've got to let me be a girl."

2

DIVERSITY

The main problem with old age was that it lasted so long. Ozzie had gotten old, in his own mind if not the general consensus, when he gave up his teaching career at seventy-five. His health then had been nearly perfect, and his mental faculties seemed intact except for some memory lapses. These things were still true five years later. What made him old wasn't his condition but his uselessness, and his problem at age eighty was knowing how long his pointless life might drag on before the world was relieved of him. His grandfather had lived to ninety-nine, and his mother had succumbed to what was normally a young person's ailment at a hundred and seven. So even though he had never avoided the various life-shortening vices that were now considered practically sacrilegious, he might have to carry on for another three decades. When he complained of this to the few old cronies he saw occasionally, they would say that longevity was better than nonexistence, whereupon he would reply that he already was nonexistent.

Ozzie hadn't exactly been forced out of his teaching job, but a day had come when he'd seen the writing on the whiteboard. Having been born a few years before the end of the previous century, he belonged to a generation subsequently known as the last children of the patriarchy. He and his male peers had spent their youth acquiring ways of thinking and acting that even then were being revealed as authoritarian. Thus when the population became effectively divided into Victims and Oppressors, Ozzie and his ilk found themselves relegated to the latter group. Becoming a high-school teacher was a poor choice under these circumstances, but for half a century he made the best of it. He was good at explaining subject matter; he handled technological innovations well enough; and he forced himself to accept whatever new teaching methods and philosophies came along. Yet after age seventy he started getting inflexible and intransigent, and what sometimes emerged were the unacceptable attitudes of his youth. In due course the kids were onto him, so it was time to quit before his classes broke into open rebellion. A year later he took a job clerking in a convenience store as a way of passing the time and supplementing his inadequate pension. Since then he'd been "promoted" to the day shift, which at least reduced the risk of getting hurt or killed in a robbery.

Ozzie's one legacy to the teaching profession was his daughter. Cynthia was forty years old and had been teaching in middle school for fifteen or sixteen years. By all indications she was very good at it, and even though he knew her career choice had little to do with him, Ozzie couldn't help feeling proud of her. In contrast to Ozzie she was well-adapted to the contemporary world and handled its educational demands with aplomb.

When Cynthia was six years old, her mother had left her for Ozzie to raise, saying he hadn't done his share of parenting during the key formative years and therefore should finish the job on his own. Accepting these terms of separation turned out to be one of the few good decisions Ozzie ever made, because having Cynthia under his wing served to anchor his life and become a source of quiet joy. Ozzie never remarried, and Cynthia stayed single as well, and even as he entered old age they continued to live together. He kept on doing the same things he always had, including all the serious cooking, and they still relied a good deal on each other for companionship. Their times together provided Ozzie's only relief from feelings of uselessness.

One evening they got home from their respective jobs at about the same time and settled into conversation over a pot of tea. Cynthia had a problem she wanted to discuss.

"One of my students has developed a serious crush on me," she said. "It's almost more than a crush. Ze keeps following me around and finding excuses to put zir hands on me."

"Please dump the post-gender references and talk the way a geezer can understand. Is this love-struck student a male?"

"Yes, a thirteen-year-old boy named Jamal. He's rather small but seems physically mature."

"Surely the standard ways of brushing off a student's attention should deal with him."

"They could probably get him away from me, but in this particular case they could expose me to charges of sexism and racism. There's also another kind of danger."

"Sexism? I thought only males could be sexist."

"You're hopelessly behind the times, Pop. For the sake of ideological purity the counter-gender paradigm has to go both ways. Girls of Jamal's age can and do touch anybody, pretty much whenever they like. Denying this latitude to a boy could be called discriminatory. Only the prickliest of male students would level such a charge, but there's no telling about Jamal. The same applies to possible charges of racism."

"What race is Jamal? Excuse me, I should include ethnicity and religion in this question since 'racism' has been expanded to cover practically everything that can be discriminated against besides gender and sexual preference."

"Jamal is Puntash."

"Omigod... I've wondered whether you had any Puntash students. Now I see the other danger you mentioned."

"Indeed. If what they say is true, a good-looking Puntash boy Jamal's age probably belongs to someone.

And if the Puntash are as fierce as I hear, that person could pose a real threat to me. As a student of world culture, could you tell me whether the Puntash really are, you know… There are no official accounts since reporting such a thing would amount to criminal defamation."

"It's true. The Puntash—meaning the males—are dedicated pederasts. This tradition goes back for centuries. They call it *bacha bazi*, or 'boy play,' and excuse it from Islamic prohibitions by saying that it isn't homosexuality so long as nobody falls in love. After all these generations, the practitioners have generally lost sexual interest in females. Hence the saying, 'for children, a woman; for pleasure, a boy.' Actually, I think this motto was once quite popular throughout the Ottoman Empire. But now it's mostly associated with the Puntash. At any rate it says that your impact on Jamal is doubly culpable; you have attracted his attention not only to the wrong person but the wrong gender."

"How do the Puntash get away with pederasty in this country?"

"Research. Many research projects—conducted by parties other than the Puntash themselves, who aren't into such things—have shown that the will to pederasty is just as deep and strong and enduring as any other sexual orientation. Its bearer is truly 'born this way,' so under today's principles its practice should be no less free of condemnation and constraint than other bodily impulses. This is why a little-noticed action by a recent federal administration expanded the acronym covering specially protected sexual practices to LGBTP, where the P is for pederast. Another quiet step taken at that time, following a precedent set by turn-of-the-century Holland, consisted of lowering the age of consent for male-male relationships to twelve. Hence Jamal would be a perfectly legal *bacha*. Two years ago he wouldn't have been, but out of compassion the law winks at violations of the age limit, the way it does at multiple wives in various insular communities."

"For some years we've been admitting what seem like huge numbers of Puntash immigrants, purportedly to fulfill diversity objectives. I don't understand why we choose to let in those particular people. They're troublesome for reasons going well beyond pederasty, and other groups from the Middle East have given us problems enough. In fact I've never understood the whole commitment to diversity—why it has been pursued so doggedly for so long."

There was a pause while Cynthia realized what she'd done. History was Ozzie's field, and cultural history was his special interest, and after his departure from teaching he rarely got a chance to show off his knowledge. Cynthia took some more tea and settled herself comfortably for the duration.

"Diversity was erected as a social goal by feminists around the time I was born," said Ozzie, settling himself as well. "Its pursuit was part of the war against patriarchy and arose from an almost hysterical belief that since gender relations in our culture were so bad, other cultures and other men had to be better. This was accompanied by a variety of academic attempts to show that patriarchy was just an aberration of recent history, a divergence from our natural condition that bore some misguided linkage to the pursuit of material advancement.

"These perspectives didn't last very long. By the early years of this century there was a grudging acknowledgement that nearly all contemporary cultures were at least as patriarchal as ours, and that throughout history patriarchal arrangements had been roughly as universal as the incest taboo. Yet the commitment to diversity didn't go away. One reason was the realization that exposure to foreignness could destabilize indigenous males regardless of its content. The feminist goal was nothing less than to deconstruct our whole culture, to tear it out by its patriarchal roots, and abrasive elements could help without having significant impacts on the rebuilding process.

"Diversity also acquired a new mission. The political left realized that a true progressive hegemony couldn't be attained until the society's self-identified Victims outnumbered its designated Oppressors. Members of racial, ethnic and sexual minority groups were firmly in the former camp, and young people were natural Victims for multiple reasons. So the Victim side would firmly take over once a majority of women—in whose image society was being transformed—came to think of themselves in those terms. But the mass of women proved slow to capture, so the interim approach was to bolster the membership of minority groups. This meant, and still means, facilitating immigration in the name of diversity.

"Like other minority-group members, immigrants will readily support measures embodying the key elements of social feminization—such as compassion, relativism, permissiveness, free expression and so forth—even though their personal lives may express diametrically opposing values. They will do this so long as their minority status delivers economic and political sweeteners, which is more or less assured by the egalitarian and compensatory features of a progressive package. The one danger is that immigrants and their descendants will stop acting and thinking like minorities. Thus, whereas we once sought immigrants who would socially assimilate, we now concentrate on those who won't.

"Which brings us to the Middle East. For centuries the residents of this area have mostly spent their time memorizing religious scriptures rather than learning how to do anything productive besides basic resource extraction. When admitted to this country, they band together in enduring, tightly knit communities that only interact with the larger society as needed to register self-interest and enjoy the benefits of a functioning economy. This makes them perfect as progressive political agents. They also serve indirectly by joining with other minority groups in defaming our attenuated complement of male Oppressors. The difficulty, of course, is that Middle Eastern immigrants have a recurring tendency to blow up and otherwise attack random members of the mainstream population. I'll have to digress a minute on how and why we've chosen to deal with this problem.

"The problem revolves around Islam. A key aspect of this religion is that it's antithetical to the development of any ironic sense. Call a Muslim violent and he'll kill you, or at least rough you up. On a larger scale this lack of ironic sense explains why Muslims feel justified in punishing us—Westerners—for criticizing Islam when its adherents keep killing us in its name. Under progressive principles the only way out of such a vicious circle is understanding, and in this case the understanding obviously has to come from the West. So given an assumption that a Muslim living here is no more dangerous to us than one living abroad, plus an assumption that cultural outreach and implicit bribes can best be applied close at hand, we've chosen to admit lots of Middle Easterners despite the associated hazards. And gradually our strategy of appeasement has paid off. At one time our casualties due to explosions and mass shootings and ritual beheadings by persons who could-have-been-but-weren't identified as Muslims numbered well up in the thousands per year, whereas now we're down to mere hundreds.

"Our policy has also involved an historical obligation. Back at the turn of the century, the residents of most Middle Eastern countries lived without complaint under the kinds of government they deserved, namely authoritarian regimes run by firm, hands-on dictators. Then came the second-worst president in

American history. After sponsoring irresponsible tax cuts that left the domestic economy in a fiscal straitjacket for decades, he plunged the U.S. into Middle Eastern wars—ostensibly to serve larger objectives but actually to avenge the actions of a few individuals—which ignited further conflicts and left the region in perpetual turmoil. At first the resulting swarms of refugees headed mainly for Europe because it was relatively close, but later they turned our way. We were more or less obliged to take them because the mess was ours.

"Last came the Puntash. They lived in such a remote part of the Middle East that the most intense fighting largely passed them by. What finally drove them out in large numbers was a precipitous decline in the price of their only resource—opium—due to the worldwide legalization of drugs. One would have thought that even an enlightened U.S. administration could have found excuses for turning away such an unsavory people, but apparently the Puntash had to be admitted as a matter of principle.

"This gets us back to your current predicament. I'm pretty familiar with the Puntash, by the way, because a lot of them come into my store."

"You've never mentioned them."

"That's because I try to think about them as little as possible. They've left me with some unforgettable images. Just yesterday, for example, I looked up from whatever I was reading at the register to see a Puntash male of about thirty waiting to pay for something. He was accompanied by his *bacha* and was passing the time by fondling the boy, who looked somewhat younger than your Jamal. On the man's face was a wide, beatific smile, and down below was an erection that was about to split his pants. He wasn't the slightest bit embarrassed. Instead he seemed quite proud of himself, or at least proud of his erection.

"At moments like this I have to be extremely careful not to evince any shock or disapproval, because the Puntash can fly from one passion to another in a heartbeat, and the only thing they enjoy more than *bacha bazi* is seeking vengeance for real or imagined slights. No insult or other offense is too small to be avenged. So if I had shown a distaste, or even a lack of appreciation, for yesterday's erection I would have risked getting carved up on the spot. Such things make me very nervous. The only upside to having the Puntash in my store is that they never steal anything. They consider it immoral.

"But yesterday's episode has gotten me thinking about what you might do. Since the Puntash are so open about their habits and proclivities, your best bet with Jamal might be to speak frankly. Get him aside and ask him point-blank whether he's got a keeper, or whatever one calls a partner in *bacha bazi*. My guess is that if he does, he'll say so. Then you ask him, more or less rhetorically, whether his displays of affection for you are putting you in danger of retribution from his significant other. How could he do this if he cares about you? Surely he can see the need, for your sake, to cool it and act like a normal thirteen-year-old boy (ha-ha). You can think of ways to make this a touching appeal."

"I don't much like the idea. You talk as if the given conversation with Jamal would be easy, but I would find it terribly awkward. Besides, suppose your 'guess' is wrong. Suppose Jamal lies and says he hasn't got a keeper even though he does."

"Well, the Puntash are certainly capable of lying, but I don't think it's likely in this case. Jamal won't hesitate to admit having a keeper if he does because it would be a point of pride. Remember, all the male Puntash—keepers and boys alike—think their system is tops and feel special about being part of it. Don't look so incredulous; the ancient Greeks thought the same thing. But the important point here is that you've got nothing to lose. Whether or not Jamal says he has a keeper, and whether or not he agrees to leave you alone, you're going to follow up by doing whatever it takes to end his advances. Talking to him will just give you an extra angle. It might also suggest other ways of proceeding."

"Okay, I'll consider it."

The next day Cynthia was late getting home and arrived looking tense and flustered. She drifted around the house for a while, then sat down over tea with an obvious intention to avoid the subject of Jamal.

"I'm getting to be a really good handicapper," she said. "In fact today was something of a triumph. The reason, or one reason, I came home late was that I had to administer a mid-term exam. This posed the usual problem of creating a level playing field."

"You mean level," said Ozzie, "in the sense that all the grades came out essentially the same."

"Right. What's making this result especially tough to achieve is that the testing modules in the new teaching software make it impossible to tinker with grades after the fact. The answers supplied by a student are either correct or they aren't, and the grades computed on that basis are automatically entered into the system with no allowance for instructor input. Given the inevitably huge variation in student proficiencies, administering these tests without some sort of intervention would yield so much grade inequality that the offending teacher would get drummed out of the profession.

"Some of my colleagues deal with the situation by supplying their students with answers to all or nearly all of the questions on a test while it's underway. The resulting grades are happily bunched together, but they don't vary much from a hundred. This draws criticism from the administration, which wants the grades clustered at some level that's not implausibly high. The craftier teachers respond by engineering their courses from the outset to deal with the grading problem. The software we're using prevents intervention in the testing process but not the presentation of subject matter, so what these teachers do is delete some judiciously chosen portion of the material to be covered by a given test. Let's say they delete ten percent of it and never mention this material in class. Then when students are tested on the whole curriculum and supplied with answers to the part they've seen, everybody comes out with a score of ninety, or a bit below that if they haven't managed to copy all the answers right.

"I've come up with a better way. It's more complicated and risky, but it eases my conscience by letting me teach courses in their entirety. What I do is extrapolate from the longstanding practice of giving extra time on tests to students with actual or purported disabilities. I assign my students to a lot of different groups, based on what I already know about their aptitudes and study habits, then vary the amounts of test-taking time across all the groups. For a test that the software says should occupy an hour, the group with my best students might get only thirty minutes. The next groups in descending order of ability might get forty minutes, fifty minutes, and so forth up to two hours. This sequencing per se wouldn't fully solve the grading problem because the worst students couldn't get acceptable grades if given forever. So I make each group leave the room when its time is up, then supply the remaining students with the answers to some questions. Succeeding groups get the answers to more and more questions, including easier and easier ones, until even the sluggards bringing up the rear can come out looking good.

"What makes this approach risky is that giving students different amounts of test-taking time could bring charges of unfairness. Unless, that is, the resulting grades are all virtually the same. It's a dictum of modern social policy that what matters is equality of outcomes, not opportunities, so if I'm a good enough handicapper to achieve that, I'm home free. The scores on the test I administered today ranged from ninety-one-point-six to ninety-three-point-two."

"Bravo. But what about Jamal? Did you talk to him?"

"Yes, I did. Jamal was in the last group to finish the test, so I got him to stick around when the other students left. Then I sat him down and did pretty much what you suggested. He understood right away when I asked whether he had a keeper—for which he used some unpronounceable Puntash word—and readily admitted that he belonged to somebody named Abdul. He spent a good deal of time bragging about what a prominent man Abdul was and how much power he wielded in the local Puntash community. Finally I got him to focus on my situation and consider the risk he was creating for me. In response he gave me a sly look suggesting he'd already thought about that. It was as if he'd been expecting me to bring up the subject, because he was ready to offer me a deal. There was something specific he wanted me to do, which wouldn't take any time or effort. If I complied with his request he would leave me completely alone thereafter.

"Talking about this is going to be really difficult. I'm not sure how much you know about FGM, female genital mutilation, which happens to be a subject I researched a few years ago. It's practiced in varying degrees by different Puntash tribes. I gather from the revolting things Jamal told me today that his group practices the most extreme version of genital cutting, which basically leaves an aperture and takes away everything else. I suppose it's only fair. The men don't enjoy sex with women, so they need to make sure the women won't enjoy sex with them.

"What this means for Jamal is that he's never seen a genitally intact female. It sounds as if he's done a good deal of looking. Puntash women are used to being treated as mere objects, so I guess getting them to expose themselves wouldn't be hard. Within the family, anything goes. But because the girls are cut at an early age, Jamal has never managed to get the true picture. That's what he wants now. From me.

"He's got the experience all planned out. The two of us would stay late after school and then go into one of the bathrooms. There I would uncover my lower body, sit on one of the toilets, and spread my legs for his inspection. It's unclear whether Jamal's motivation is prurience or simple curiosity. I can't decide which is worse.

"You are <u>not</u> going to do that!"

"My response exactly. But Jamal didn't seem at all fazed by this reaction. He sort of smirked and said if I chose not to comply, he might not be able to keep Abdul from finding out about 'us.' He even implied that he might let Abdul believe I'd been leading him on.

"Before you start pounding the table, keep in mind the kind of danger involved. The police aren't about to do anything based on such a veiled threat, and the possibility of punishment after the fact won't necessarily keep Abdul from coming after me. You know as well as I do that once their blood is up, the Puntash don't give much of a damn about consequences. Furthermore Abdul might even get away with killing me, if he arranges to do it on Puntash turf where the action would be covered by sharia law. Maybe he'd just have to give some camels to my next of kin. You could ride one of them to work every day. Or maybe he could present his action as an 'honor killing' and get off scot-free.

"I've gone around and around trying to think of some counter-threat. All I've come up with is one slim reed. While Jamal and I were talking, I noticed that he kept shifting around uncomfortably in his seat. Then I recalled seeing him do this in class over the last few days. So I suspect he's got an itch or some other aggravation on his bottom. What I'm hearing about their activities would suggest that Puntash boys can develop real problems down there."

"Right. I once heard a Puntash man in my store complain in English that his young companion was out of action due to 'bacha bum'."

"Thus my thought was that I could threaten to take Jamal to the school nurse for an inspection. The nurse is a woman, and any Puntash male would find it utterly humiliating to be physically examined by a female. Jamal might consider the idea so repulsive that he'd agree openly or tacitly to leave me alone. A big concern, however, is that even with such an agreement Jamal might send Abdul after me just for spite. This afternoon's talk revealed how ugly he can get."

"You may be onto something. Let's say that Jamal really does have an issue with his bottom. If so, it's probably something infectious. Keep in mind that, whereas our politicians and law enforcers are terrified of offending the Puntash, our public health agencies are an empire unto themselves. They're hell on communicable diseases, and they don't care whom they offend. So if the school nurse found that Jamal had an infectious condition related to all the *bazi* going on, she would immediately bring in other public health people, who would make him identify his sexual partners and demand to inspect them as well. They could track down Abdul even if Jamal wouldn't name him, and they've got the police powers necessary to force Abdul into a physical exam."

"I don't see how threatening to put this in motion would improve matters. Being forcibly examined wouldn't exactly make Abdul happy. If anything it would increase the chance of his coming after me. I can imagine Jamal pointing this out, with a smile on his face, and calling my bluff."

"But I'm not talking about a threat. I think you should go through with what you've described. Tomorrow, without warning, get Jamal hauled out of class and taken to the school nurse for a physical exam. If she finds something infectious, the public health agencies will go after Abdul as I've said. Events can then unfold in various ways, and some of the possibilities might be helpful. Abdul might be so enraged by the physical exam he forgets about you, if at that point he even knows about you. Or he might be placed in quarantine for an extended period while undergoing treatment. Either way the public health people will have your back, more or less. I just think you'll be best off perturbing the situation rather than letting things play out as they stand, although it's a gamble."

Cynthia and Ozzie discussed the matter well into the evening, with Cynthia eventually saying she would take her father's advice. The decisive factor was that Jamal had insisted on hearing the next day whether she would accede to his intrusive demand. Cynthia felt she had to do something—anything—rather than give him an answer.

The next day Ozzie got home from work at his usual hour and waited anxiously for Cynthia to appear. For a long time she didn't. He started calling her number, to no avail, and tried to calm himself by taking care of little tasks around the house. He was sitting at a table doing nothing when Cynthia finally arrived. Her face was drawn, practically haggard, but she looked calm and possibly relieved. Without asking, Ozzie set aside his own tea and fixed them both martinis. He had poured their second drinks by the time Cynthia was ready to talk.

"A lot has happened. I suppose everything turned out well, although the whole experience was unsettling to say the least. To start at the beginning, I dropped by the infirmary before classes to have a talk with Betty—the school nurse, who happens to be a good friend. She was immediately concerned when I told her my suspicions about Jamal, because several venereal diseases have recently broken out among our students. She agreed right away to have Jamal brought in for examination as soon as possible, saying she would give me a report later in the day.

"Betty got back to me during lunch hour. Two security officers had extracted Jamal from one of his early classes and forced him to let Betty inspect him in the infirmary. Betty said the visual signs were obvious and were clearly confirmed by a bacteriological test, for which she's got some diagnostic kit that yields results right away. Jamal has anorectal gonorrhea. This is taken very seriously because the bacterium involved has developed resistance to most antibiotics and responds poorly to the ones that work at all.

"Betty then moved just as forcefully as you predicted, directing the security officers to keep Jamal under guard while she summoned three people from the public health agencies. Once on the scene the agency people grilled Jamal about his sexual partners, but he refused to tell them anything. They were quite interested, however, when I passed along the word that Jamal's keeper was somebody named Abdul. They said this would give them a start. Two of them took Jamal off to be quarantined in some county facility, while the third left to organize a search for the relevant Abdul. This was how matters stood at lunchtime. I thanked Betty a lot for her involvement, although this obviously wasn't necessary, and practically begged her to keep me apprised of further developments. I'm sure she could tell that I had something particular at stake in the situation, but she's the kind of friend who wouldn't ask.

"Betty met me again at the end of classes and said I had to go someplace with her. She's a person who won't take no for an answer, so I grabbed my belongings and followed her out of the building. On the way she explained that Jamal's keeper Abdul had been found and was being held at a location we would reach shortly. The parties holding him included three public health workers and roughly a half-dozen police officers. Betty had convinced the health people that she should do the testing of Abdul because she had a portable diagnostic kit and was more up-to-speed on venereal diseases than anyone else on hand. Furthermore she had insisted on bringing me along, for which she pinned some sort of badge on me that matched one she was wearing.

"I don't know whether you've ever been in our local Puntash enclave, but let me just say that I found the experience shocking. The garbage, the noise, the swarming children, the goats. In the space of a block I felt as if I'd gone three centuries, or maybe a dozen centuries, back in time. Anyway we walked through a gate in a wall and crossed a courtyard full of drying laundry and goat poop. A doorway on the far side opened onto a large, dim and dusty room. There we found Abdul being restrained by four police officers and shouting Puntash imprecations at the top of his lungs. He was a big man, about forty, with furious beady eyes and enormous moustaches.

"Adding to the bedlam were Abdul's three wives. As was explained to me later by a police officer I'll be mentioning, even the most ardent practitioners of *bacha bazi* have female wives as well. They see no conflict, and neither do the wives. These particular women were all screaming in Puntash and running around the room flapping their burqas. Given their head-to-toe coverage we could only tell that one wife was enormously fat and one was vanishingly thin. Their anger was directed at all the intruders but seemed to find a special focus in Betty and me. I was getting more and more afraid until some police officers managed to lever the wives out of the room. Meanwhile the other officers were dealing with Abdul's garments and wrestling him into position for inspection.

"Betty did her job while Abdul howled. Then she used her diagnostic kit to reveal: nothing. Abdul was clean. Much to my surprise, getting the word that he was okay didn't calm him down. If anything his fury increased, although he became less threatening to the people who'd been holding him.

"During this episode I noticed that one of the police officers was able to understand Puntash, so once we were safely outside I asked him what had been going on with Abdul, who apparently knew some English but never used it. The explanation was simple enough. Abdul was mad about being free of gonorrhea because this meant Jamal had been infected by somebody else. The little devil had been two-timing him. The outbursts we heard from Abdul after his test were graphic descriptions of what he was going to do to Jamal in retribution.

"So there we are. Unless Abdul has already heard somehow about Jamal's attachment to a teacher, there's no longer any danger to me, because I'm sure nothing Jamal says from now on can direct Abdul's anger away from Jamal himself. I seem to be in the clear."

Ozzie and Cynthia had another drink to celebrate, then went to bed. The next two days passed without incident. But on the following day, a Friday, Cynthia didn't come home at all. Ozzie called her repeatedly throughout the evening and slept very little that night. The next day, lacking any other ideas, he retraced the route she always used when walking to and from work. A few of the people he met could recall seeing her pass by occasionally, but nobody had noticed her or seen anything suspicious the day before. Upon returning home, Ozzie got the idea of calling Betty, whom he had never met but who might understand his special reasons for concern. He located her number in one of Cynthia's files and got an answer right away. Betty listened attentively while he explained that, while Cynthia sometimes stayed overnight with one of her male friends, she never-ever did this without notifying Ozzie. Many days would pass before the police took any action on a missing person report for a normally responsible forty-year-old, and given the ominous circumstances involving Jamal, Ozzie didn't think he could afford to wait.

"I agree that this is serious," said Betty, cutting him off. "Some things have happened with Jamal that may be relevant. He was in quarantine at the county until Thursday. I got the people there to let me supervise his case and take over the effort to find out his sexual partners. He got very scared on hearing about the scene with Abdul, and when given a promise of release if he cooperated, he finally broke down and said that his other paramour had been somebody named Omar Shadoof. I then let him go and had the county health people send out a team in search of this Omar.

"The team hadn't caught up with Omar as of yesterday afternoon, but by interviewing some kids in Abdul's neighborhood they got an idea of what was happening. It seems that Abdul has sworn blood vendettas against both Jamal and Omar, whom he has somehow identified as Jamal's back-door man. The kids were pretty certain that Abdul wouldn't kill both of them. He would slaughter whichever one he encountered first and then make peace with the other. In any case, while Abdul is chasing around looking for his two targets, Omar is avoiding him and the health people while seeking Jamal. Apparently Omar is a believer in democracy, because what he wants is to have Jamal choose between him and Abdul. If Jamal chooses Abdul as his true love, Omar will go away, but given an opposite choice he'll confront Abdul and fight it out.

"I'm going to help you go after Cynthia," continued Betty, "and maybe I can bring in somebody else. I'll call you back."

The return call came fifteen minutes later. "I've been talking to Detective Officer Bopp of the local police. He was the Puntash-speaking member of our party last week who explained to Cynthia what was happening with Abdul. He has taken a romantic interest in her, which I know because he called me later to ask for her number. Bopp has struck me as the altruistic type, so given his weakness for Cynthia I thought he might be willing to help, and indeed he is. But without the cover of a health mission he can't enter the Puntash enclave as a police officer. He'll have to go unarmed and out of uniform."

Betty said their meeting place would be the point where she had entered the Puntash enclave to conduct Abdul's test. Bopp felt they should proceed from there on foot. Ozzie estimated how long it would take him to reach the given point, and they set their meeting time accordingly.

Ozzie found Betty to be an agreeable but no-nonsense woman of middle age and physically commanding presence. Officer Bopp was tall, thin, and milder in aspect than Ozzie expected of a policeman. The three of them conferred for a minute at their meeting point. Lacking any other place to start their search, they would go first to Abdul's residence. They couldn't imagine any reason why Abdul would be holding Cynthia captive, but they felt obliged to assume an abduction rather than something worse, and the only threats to Cynthia revolved around Abdul. Possibly they could get some information from neighborhood kids the way the health team had done.

For their enclave, the Puntash had taken over an area with a regular street grid like the rest of the city, but all the roads had been transformed by spillovers of activity and debris from the adjacent buildings. The sidewalks and pavement were littered with tables, chairs, vendors, loiterers, screaming children, and wandering animals to such extent that only the nimblest vehicles could weave through. The passage of Ozzie, Betty and Bopp attracted curious stares, with noticeable hostility toward Betty because her face and head were uncovered. In a fairly short time they reached Abdul's street and confronted the high wall that bordered his whole property. The gate was closed. Without hesitation Betty tried its handle and found it locked.

There was an overflowing trash bin by the wall near the gate, so Officer Bopp said he might as well climb up and take a look. He raised himself just high enough to see over the wall. After holding this position for a protracted moment, he ducked down so suddenly that he lost his footing and fell into the garbage next to the bin. Some time passed while he collected himself, since he was clearly shaken by his findings as well as his fall. What had startled him was that Abdul had stepped through a doorway into the courtyard bearing a huge knife. But before then Bopp had been able to see through the same doorway into the room where Betty had done her testing. And there he had spotted Cynthia, clearly alive but tied to a chair against the far wall.

While describing this scene, Bopp recalled that there was a window in the wall behind Cynthia, just above one of her shoulders. The group then considered the possibility that this window opened onto an alleyway they could enter. If so, they might use it to communicate with Cynthia before deciding what to do. They walked to one end of the block, then took a side street to find that there was indeed an alley behind the houses. Bopp led the group down this debris-choked passage and located the relevant window, based on his memory of its dimensions and a reckoning of distances.

Ozzie was trembling with worry and insisted on being the one to make contact. As far as he could see through the window, there was nobody in the room besides Cynthia. He spoke loudly enough to get her attention and found that she was fully alert. Their first words back and forth were hurried expressions of relief and anxiety. Then Ozzie said that Betty and Officer Bopp were with him and asked why in the world Abdul was holding her.

"Abdul isn't the one holding me," said Cynthia. "He just came home for lunch. By now he has probably headed out again to resume his search for Jamal and Jamal's other boyfriend. The people who brought me here and are now holding me are Abdul's three wives.

"One of the wives has a six-year-old daughter who speaks English and has been happy to explain everything. Apparently when Jamal was lounging around here last week on a visit with Abdul, he idly mentioned to one of the wives that he planned to make a teacher at school show him what an uncut woman looked like. Then when Betty and I and the others were here for Abdul's test, the wives asked Officer Bopp about me and found out I was one of Jamal's teachers. Somehow these circumstances convinced the wives—who aren't very bright—that I was the person wanting to have Abdul tested. The only possible reason would be that I was planning to have sex with him. This really sent the wives into a tizzy. A *bacha* or two is neither here nor there, but a female rival would be intolerable.

"The wives don't intend to kill me. Apparently they've gotten Jamal's and Abdul's perspectives mixed up and decided that Abdul wants me because I'm uncut. So they intend to take away this factor. The only reason my cutting ceremony hasn't happened yet is that the wives are waiting to borrow a special implement for the job, which apparently circulates around the neighborhood on an as-needed basis. But the six-year-old, who was recently cut herself, says I haven't got a thing to worry about."

"Do you have any idea how we can set you free?" asked Ozzie.

"There's a back door from the alley into the kitchen, which is the next room down from here. This door is always left open to let the goats go in and out. It's hard to say how many wives you'll encounter if you use it. They've been periodically leaving the house today, which I know because they're all wearing their burqas. It's also hard to know what kind of a fight they'll put up. They're very savage people, but they don't seem to carry weapons. The most important question is whether Abdul will be around. If he finds you liberating me, he might shrug and let me go, or he might chop off all of your heads, depending on his mood or perhaps what he's had for lunch."

Ozzie turned from the window to find that Betty and Bopp had taken cover behind a pile of broken furniture because they'd seen some women using the alleyway further down. He joined them and recounted what he'd heard from Cynthia. There was an immediate decision that all three of them would go in the kitchen door and take their chances with any resistance. They waited until the one woman currently in the alley had departed from its far end, then made their move.

Betty took the lead. Her entry into the kitchen brought a shriek from one of the wives, who'd been stirring a cauldron full of some vile-smelling liquid. This wife—the skinny one—took the ladle she'd been holding and ran forth while raising it to strike. Betty managed to grab it coming down, but the ladle was too hot to hold, leaving her no choice but to flee around the kitchen. By this time Officer Bopp had entered and run into the fat wife, who was screaming at the top of her lungs and brandishing a heavy frying pan. She was a titanic figure, and Bopp was only able to avoid her wild swings of the pan by nimbly interposing several of the goats that were eating something off the kitchen floor. Meanwhile Ozzie had ducked past the action and run into the main room to untie Cynthia.

Presently the swings of the ladle by the skinny wife cooled it down enough for Betty to hold, whereupon she grabbed it and wrestled it away. During the ensuing struggle one of the two women, it wasn't clear which, tripped over a goat and brought both of them falling through the doorway into the main room. By then Officer Bopp had already retreated through this doorway to gain maneuvering space in his flight from the fat wife and her frying pan. Ozzie was kneeling by Cynthia's chair and finding it difficult to untie her knots.

The skinny wife proved to be no match for Betty once she was unarmed and sprawling on the floor. Her greatest disadvantage turned out to be that her diminutive frame didn't come close to filling out her burqa, which left her wallowing in great folds of heavy fabric. Betty deftly pushed her head down into the body of this tent and got her arms mostly out of the sleeves, which were promptly tied together. The skinny wife was then more or less entombed in her burqa, and when Betty let her go she started flopping around on the floor like a heffalump trying to get out.

Meanwhile Bopp was encountering a new difficulty with the fat wife. Having established that she couldn't get close enough to hit him with the frying pan, she had tossed that aside and picked up a hookah from someplace in the room. It was a hookah of magnitude, with four long tubes extending from its upper part to accommodate multiple smokers. She wielded it effortlessly and started twirling it in tight circles over her head. The fixture holding the tubes was apparently designed to rotate, because the tubes were soon whizzing around like helicopter blades. The mouthpieces at the ends of the tubes weren't heavy, but they were moving at terrific speed and posed a serious threat to Officer Bopp as the fat wife waddled after him.

Bopp was just managing to stay out of range when he stepped in a pile of goat poop and went down. Being challenged in terms of deceleration as well as acceleration, the fat wife got tangled in Bopp's feet and went down on top of him, knocking him momentarily senseless. She then kept him pinned to the floor with her massive corporeality while trying to wrap one of the tubes of the hookah around his neck.

Betty was on her way across the floor to help Bopp when she heard a new shriek and turned to face its source. Standing in the doorway from the kitchen was the third wife, the middle-sized one, with rage in her eyes and a frightful implement in her hand. Betty knew in a flash that this implement could only be the neighborhood's genital mutilator, which the given wife had finally managed to borrow for application to Cynthia. It was about the size of a garden trowel, with a wickedly curving blade at its end and some little scoopers and scrapers along the sides. Holding the mutilator out in front of her at crotch level, the middle-sized wife began a snarling advance toward Betty.

Betty was jumping back from the third lunge of the genital mutilator when she bumped into the encapsulated body of the skinny wife, which by then had worked its way out to the middle of the floor. Flailing movements inside this cocoon caused Betty to flip over and land head-first on the floor. As she was rolling over and trying to clear her head, there came a masculine bellow from the doorway to the courtyard. It was Abdul, home for prayers but now shaking with fury and holding an uplifted scimitar. The blade of this fearsome weapon rose in a cruel arc nearly three feet long that gleamed mercilessly in the sunlight from the courtyard. Having recognized Betty as the woman who had humiliated him in this very room, Abdul was about to take his revenge.

But as the scimitar came down, a goat wandered forward to sniff Betty's hair and took the blow instead. It was a textbook decapitation, from which the goat's head rolled merrily across the room to get entangled in the tubes of the fat wife's hookah, but it changed everything. The middle-sized wife dropped her mutilator and wailed tearfully because the given animal had been her favorite. Meanwhile Abdul recoiled in the knowledge that he had just slaughtered a perfectly good goat, which under Islamic law had to be eaten. To pretend that its preparation had been halal, he uttered the holy word *bismillah* while convincing himself that the goat's head had been properly aligned with Mecca. Then he rushed the body into the kitchen to drain its blood.

Betty wasted no time in picking up the genital mutilator and advancing on the middle-sized wife with a murderous look in her eyes. She slammed the given wife against a wall and held her there with a forearm while inserting the tip of the mutilator into one nostril. Then she proceeded to raise this device very slowly, a millimeter at a time. The other woman's eyes were popping out in terror and her tiptoes had reached their ultimate limit when two other things happened.

First Abdul came into the room, having finished bleeding his goat, and rushed to pick up his scimitar where it had been dropped. Then another man appeared in the doorway to the courtyard. It was Omar Shadoof, holding a scimitar in one hand and Jamal's arm in the other. Jamal had been forced to make a choice, and Omar had been declared his favorite, so Omar had arrived to make Abdul accept that Jamal would no longer be his *bacha*. Threats and insults followed, and scimitars were raised, and the battle was on.

Abdul was the bigger man and was presumably more experienced, but Omar was about fifteen years younger and clearly more agile. Between their two awesome scimitars there was little to choose. Both of the warriors fought right-handed. Abdul swung first and clearly intended to go on the offensive. Omar fell into a pattern of strategic retreat, blocking or dodging Abdul's efforts while looking for a clear opening. Neither party had drawn blood when the fighting moved near the courtyard door and Abdul landed a tremendous blow on one of the doorposts. His blade apparently went all the way through the post, but he managed to wrench it out quickly. This action pulled the top of the post askew, however, so that the lintel above the doorway and part of the overlying wall dropped a few inches. Since the wall consisted largely of some granular material like stucco, its disturbance released a thick cloud of dust. Visibility in the nearby part of the room dropped to a foot or two.

The dust cloud denied the onlookers the sight of a perfect *pas de deux*. Each warrior thought that the haze was rendering the other one unprepared. Abdul held his left arm out for balance and raised his scimitar up to deliver a curving stroke, down and across. At that moment Omar was doing precisely the same thing. They swung at exactly the same time and decapitated each other. The heads landed in synchrony as the bodies collapsed. Abdul's middle-sized wife, whom Betty had released while watching the swordplay, picked up his head to make sure he was dead. And that was that.

There was nothing left to fight about, so as the dust cloud settled, Betty assisted the fat wife in rolling off of Bopp while the middle-sized wife helped free the skinny one from her burqa. Meanwhile Jamal took over for Ozzie, who had never succeeded in getting Cynthia's ropes untied. Jamal felt bad about all the trouble he'd caused Cynthia and was only too glad to help. Once liberated, Cynthia leapt up and, slipping past her father, fell into the arms of Officer Bopp.

So the group's brush with diversity turned out well enough. Jamal had to find another source of *bazi* and Ozzie needed a new companion for tea, but Cynthia and Bopp were an item.

3

CHANGE AGENT

"Well hello Sugar! I was hoping you'd drop by. Today was your lunch with Jeckleburg, right? Give me credit—not many people could've gotten you in with him. Anyway you look really smashing. I've never seen you do your face like that, and the dress doesn't leave much to the imagination. You've got the chops, for sure. But maybe I should have warned you that looks only go so far with producers like Jeckleburg.

"Oh, I guess you've already discovered that. You don't seem happy with the way things went. Not happy at all. Um, hey, there-there... You should sit down... In fact why don't you lie down on the sofa while I get a hanky or something. Try to relax. Take deep breaths. Get control of yourself. Here are some tissues. Just try to keep your mascara from dripping on my suede calfskin.

"Okay, you're saying the meeting wasn't a total loss. But still you look really rejected, like a boyfriend just dumped you or something. What were you expecting? That Jeckleburg would sweep you away to his casting couch and –

"No, no, I wasn't implying that. It was just a figure of speech.

"So Jeckleburg said he liked what he saw, but he'd gotten his people to check you out, and he didn't like what he couldn't see. He was talking about your image, right? Your political image. He said you didn't have a political image, and until you did, he couldn't use you.

"It's my fault. I knew we would have a problem down the road, but didn't think Jeckleburg would pounce on it right away. You only signed on with me a couple of weeks ago, and since then I've been too busy to give you any sort of orientation. But you were obviously going to be a hot property, so I couldn't resist setting you up with Jeckleburg when I caught him at a party with his defenses down. I got carried away and forgot that you were in no shape to be exposed to anybody important, least of all him.

"Trust me, everything is recoverable. No doors have been closed, to Jeckleburg or anyone else. But we've got a lot of work to do. Or rather, you do. I can only tell you what has to happen and why. Have you got time to talk for a while?

"I gather you don't know the first thing about Hollywood. For starters, the once-famous casting couch has been gone much longer than it existed. Movie producers now build their egos in a totally different way. Money and glory are still important, but what producers go for most is self-esteem. They earn self-esteem by serving Hollywood's mission. Your job as an aspiring performer is to understand this mission and align yourself with it from head to toe.

"The mission of Hollywood is to be a change agent. This applies to the industry as a whole and to its self-esteeming participants, who see themselves as individual change agents. What's the change being sought? Progress. Meaning the advancement of progressive politics. You're surely familiar with progressive thinking. It mostly coincides with the posture called political correctness, which comes from looking at everything from a female perspective.

"What made Hollywood go left? Good question. One answer is that political correctness has basically cornered the market for self-esteem, due to the decline of religion and traditional values and so forth. Hollywood participants can't resist tapping into this source of gratification because their power to influence public opinion makes it so easy. Another answer has to do with youth. The film industry has to focus heavily on young people because they are the main ones willing to spend serious money on movie-going. Youth has always rebelled against authority, and this holds now more than ever because the weaker the authority exercised over young people growing up, the more they resent it. The anti-authoritarian impulse—which is the essence of hipness—is a core element of political correctness. Thus the film industry would be pushed in this direction by market forces if nothing else. The same factors apply to the music industry, but we needn't get into that.

"Okay, to describe how Hollywood operates as a change agent I should say something about the kinds of movies that get made. Basically there are four types, which I'll list in ascending order of service to the mission. At the bottom is a miscellaneous category containing kiddie shows, horror flicks, noir offerings, goofy comedies and other products that don't do anything but respond to market demand. Some of the kiddie shows have uplifting themes, but we may as well ignore the miscellaneous category. The others are: male fantasy movies, female fantasy movies, and uplifting movies.

"Male fantasy offerings are the films that show men as old-fashioned heroes. This genre, which basically includes all 'action' movies, is declining but still in demand. There are only limited ways in which Hollywood can bend it to serve the mission. For example, some male characters can be given feminizing vulnerabilities. Or female characters can be included among the action figures, to suggest that women can do everything men can do and that men ought to love and approve aggressive ones. What's funny is that because male viewers want these characters to be sexy, they have to see sixty-kilo women tossing around hundred-kilo men; but they're generally dumb enough to buy this. In any case little can be gained professionally or politically from appearing in these films, and you shouldn't do it unless there's nothing else available.

"Female fantasy movies are basically romances, like those in the old days except that about half of the love relationships and sex scenes are now female-female. This helps to attract male audiences because men like to watch women doing women, so they can imagine being included, even though the whole point is that they're not included. Female fantasy movies serve Hollywood's mission much better than their male counterparts because they can be more consistently affirmative. Along with celebrating sexual freedom and diversity, they can illustrate all sorts of ways in which politically correct behaviors lead to happy endings. Their male characters, if any, can teach men in the audience how to think and act like women while graciously tolerating women who act like men. With your looks, you could make it big in female fantasy, but since these products tend to be formulaic you would risk getting typecast.

"Uplifting movies are where the rubber really meets the road for Hollywood as a change agent. These products can be infinitely variable in terms of plotting, context, characters and action, but most of them boil down to classic contests between good and evil. Along with old-fashioned types of villainy, the manifestations of evil include offenses like sexism, racism, xenophobia, patriarchy, animal abuse, economic exploitation, environmental rapacity and any form of intolerance. Even after a hundred years, Nazis make the best evil-doers, although they're a bit weak on ecology. The forces of good are generally female in spirit if not in body. After surviving close calls of one kind or another, the good side prevails, showing again that political correctness is more than its own reward. Uplifting movies are the main event in this industry, tops in terms of box office and quality of roles and opportunities to live large in the public consciousness. They are where you belong, and where you'll get if you listen up.

"In thinking about what happened with Jeckleburg, you may feel that it's pointless or even impossible to develop a political image before you've got a public presence to wear it. But this isn't so. Try to imagine the grin on the disappearing Cheshire cat, with the grin coming first rather than the cat. Hollywood is full of people who're famous for being famous, and what came first was the fame, not the person. Happening to go viral in a porn video was once a good way to start, although this has now been done to death.

"By the way, you're bisexual, right?

"Never mind. That was a rhetorical question, because all women are naturally bisexual. Let me just say that you'd better get used to going both ways onscreen if you want to thrive in this business. What you do elsewhere won't matter for the moment because sexual antics can't get much up-front attention anymore.

"But you can accomplish a whole lot with words. Hollywood people are always talking, trying to impress or sell or manipulate each other, and some of them exist to report upon or gossip about the rest. With your looks you won't have much trouble getting into the places where this happens and passing yourself off as somebody important. All you'll have to do then is offer progressive sentiments in a new and quotable way.

"Here's an example. A young actress told some writer she was so committed to saving energy and fighting climate change that in the bathroom she only used one sheet—one sheet!—of toilet paper to wipe herself. National news services picked up this quote, letting the given individual simultaneously advertise her political correctness and tell the world how she managed her twat. Was that beautiful or what? The girl was on her way.

"Another example was the starlet who said she might bear children sometime but would never breast-feed them, because nursing amounted to incest. Because breasts were basically sexual organs. Notice how this gambit worked on multiple levels. It was more or less politically correct, since feminists have turned against breast-feeding in heterosexual contexts because it's gender-specific and therefore sexist. Meanwhile the statement pointed out how sexy the speaker was and advertised the allure of her boobs. Truly a tour de force. Stardom awaits.

"An example of even more advanced celebrity gamesmanship was a quote I saw recently having to do with black people's complaints about their treatment by police. In the ongoing debate about this issue, political correctness had kept everyone from mentioning the disproportionate black responsibility for crime.

But the speaker turned this fact to advantage, saying: "...blacks have little faith in a criminal justice system that imprisons them at six times the rate of whites." A positive spin would require the audience to believe that four or five of every six black inmates had been framed. The speaker didn't have to say this, however, since right-thinking listeners would reflexively and uncritically fill in the blank. An important lesson here is that celebrities are never cross-examined. They can say anything without fear of contradiction, and their opinions are always relevant because they're celebrities.

"You're undoubtedly a clever girl who can devise all sorts of verbal ploys to get attention. But once they've put you on the stage, your words should blend into actions. You must appear with high visibility in contexts that flaunt your progressive convictions. Start at low-cost locations, then expand your liberating presence to a national and eventually global scale.

"Chain yourself to a tree; lie down in front of a bulldozer; march in a left-wing demonstration; become an honorary Native American. Trust me, the cameras will find you. Over time, as you build your progressive persona, you'll want to specialize in one or two areas. The field of LGBT advocacy is now way oversubscribed, but there are plenty of other oppressed peoples to embrace. Try to pick a group that lets you call their oppressors racist, even if race isn't actually their defining factor. Avoid groups serving as negative targets, like the 'one percent' who hog all the money, because their victims can only be embraced conceptually.

"In the long run, animals are the ticket. This is a long-run focus because animals are only worth doing once you've gone global. Wolves and spotted owls and snail darters and other domestic offerings just don't measure up to the species found on other continents. One reason animals are top-of-the-line for celebrity attention is that they're so photogenic. For example, just one image of you cavorting with a family of cheetahs would suffice to put your star on the Walk of Fame. Another reason is that animal conservation has so many angles. You can fight to save elephant tusks, rhinoceros horns, shark fins, panda habitat, whatever. And if you play your cards right, nonprofit organizations will pay you to do it.

"So are you feeling better now? Never doubt that with proper self-promotion you've got the power to keep the Jeckleburgs of this business eating out of your hand. And meanwhile you'll have the quiet satisfaction of knowing that what really matters is the way you look.

4

SAFE SPACE

Spork didn't really mind being useless, since he was far from alone in this regard and could hardly remember life on other terms. Struggling to fill the time was surely better than running out of time. Spork believed he would last at least ten more years, which would give him the distinction of having lived in three different centuries. He would then be laid to rest with this as his only distinction.

Much of his time was spent reading and thinking about the state of the country. In this pastime Spork had trouble keeping his thoughts and judgments from being swayed by his own alienation from the modern world. Due to a dogged lack of interest in technology and its fruits, he had lost touch with basic elements of life: how people communicated, how they got things done, how they entertained themselves and so forth. This yielded an ongoing tendency to conclude that society had taken a wrong turn somewhere and life was going downhill. But when resisting this temptation, which was most of the time, Spork had to admit that the biggest public decisions had generally been wise.

The relentless advance of technology had raised a lot of serious issues, the most critical being its impact on employment. Automation of productive tasks had hollowed out the nation's middle class in the first half of the century by eliminating most clerical and factory jobs. Then came the so-called singularity, the point at which artificial intelligence caught up with human intelligence, which promised to eliminate more and more high-skill occupations. Employees would then fall into three sharply different categories: first, an elite group including the designers and managers of automated systems, plus some other knowledge workers and entrepreneurs, who would earn a grossly disproportionate share of all income; second, an intermediate group providing public and private services that consumers would only accept from human beings; and third, a bottom group of manual workers whose pay would be too low to justify automation. The resulting income inequality would be so severe that unless mitigated in some fashion it would yield an economic caste system with very little upward mobility.

Serious consideration was given at mid-century to suppressing applications of technology through legal means, but the leadership finally judged that such laws would yield greater economic costs than benefits, to the extent that they were enforceable at all. Proposals to place severe limits on international trade, another source of income inequality, were rejected for largely similar reasons. The country decided instead to let the economic chips fall where they might, and then to obtain a livable distribution of spending power by rearranging the results.

The primary mechanisms were progressive taxes—meaning higher amounts were taxed at higher rates—and the wage subsidy program. Progressive taxation of income had long existed, although rate schedules had to be considerably steepened. The chief innovation was the establishment of excise and property taxes on a progressive basis. The biggest source of excise tax revenue was the progressive taxation of net domestic energy use, including electricity consumption by vehicles. Other sales taxes were made progressive in cases where product cost varied mostly with quality rather than functionality. The schedule for progressive real estate taxation started at zero and held there far enough to relieve minimal dwellings of any tax liability.

The federal wage subsidy program involved the creation of a redistribution fund that operated as follows. A worker earning X after-tax dollars per hour would receive a bi-weekly payroll deposit of X plus Y dollars per hour. Y came from the redistribution fund and would decrease with higher X until it went negative and the person became a net subsidizer of others. The fund disbursed all the money it took in, and the system maintained work incentives because a person had to earn X in order to get Y. The subsidies for the lowest-paid workers—many of whom were hired by the government to perform tasks of marginal economic value—were large enough to support them adequately with very little labor market intervention.

Spork had been on all sides of the system in the course of his long life. During his professional years he earned enough to support other people via the redistribution fund but didn't manage to save much for his own retirement. Thus when the world decided his skills were obsolete, he had to fall back upon menial jobs and their accompanying subsidies. Then the death of his wife reduced his living expenses enough to let him retire altogether, given his small Social Security pension and the mercies of the National Health Service. This left him with little to do and lots of time to do it.

Spork had one child and one grandchild living together nearby. The child was a middle-aged government worker named Morgan. As a recalcitrant old-timer, Spork had reached a compromise with modern patterns of thought and language wherein he attributed gender to adults but not children. Thus he acknowledged Morgan as a daughter, and when thinking and talking about her he used the old pronouns and possessive forms associated with females. But in the case of his grandchild, an eleven-year-old named Riley, he bowed to the demands of a post-gender world and used only neutral referents.

One Friday afternoon Spork got a request from Morgan for help in looking after Riley. Morgan had just received an invitation to go somewhere with a friend for a weekend getaway. Spork knew that the friend was probably a romantic interest and could well be a woman. He had long felt rebuked by Morgan's drift toward female lovers and her failure to secure a father figure for Riley, but had learned to hold his tongue. The problem at hand was Riley's need for supervision on Saturday night and all day Sunday. Riley would be sleeping over with somebody on Friday night, but had invited two other friends to stay at zir house starting on Saturday afternoon. Ze was a generally responsible child who could manage the household safely for short periods, but the two friends—also aged around eleven—were unknown quantities, and they would have the run of the place for a full day. Thus Morgan was hoping Spork could stay over for this duration just to keep an eye on things. There would be no other duties, since the children could cook for themselves and could deploy Morgan's housebot to clean up.

Spork walked over to Morgan's residence on Saturday afternoon and found his three charges already there. Like Riley, the two friends appeared to be personable and attractive children in age-appropriate ways. Riley introduced the friends as Hunter and Carson. Hunter was tall and outspoken, whereas Carson was short and apparently shy. After a modicum of conversation, the three of them disappeared into Riley's room and left Spork to pass the time as he chose. He settled himself in the den at the front of the house to stay out of the way and happily dug into the pile of reading material he'd brought along. Soon he noticed it was raining outside, with a light shower developing into a downpour that showed no signs of abating.

In the evening Spork heard the children preparing food in the kitchen and found himself joining them. Initially he worried that his adult presence would be an unwelcome intrusion. But he quickly saw that this wouldn't apply because his unimaginable age made him a post-adult who didn't exist for the kids in any meaningful way. So he warmed up something to eat and took the fourth chair at the kitchen table. The dinnertime chatter consisted mainly of a forceful monologue from Hunter highlighted by bold assertions and sweeping generalizations. In what seemed to be a standard conversational format, Riley acted as Hunter's foil, periodically challenging zir statements and offering alternative truths. This would yield a brief argument, spirited but not ill-mannered, whereupon Hunter would re-launch zir monologue on a somewhat different tack. Carson generally kept quiet but seemed to enjoy listening.

Spork returned to the den while the talk continued in the kitchen. A good while later the kids went back to Riley's room, where an extra bed had been set up to let them all sleep there. Spork was planning to retire in Morgan's bedroom, but found that its location next to Riley's room would make going to sleep difficult. The noises coming through the wall alternated between loud talking, quiet talking, various kinds of bumping around, and no noise at all. The intermittent periods of silence turned out to be the most unnerving, even though Spork told himself that they were just intervals when the group members were all occupied with electronic amusements. At length he got up from Morgan's bed and returned to the front of the house, where he lay down on a long sofa in the living room. The rain was still coming down heavily when he fell asleep.

He was sitting over a last cup of coffee when the kids emerged in mid-morning. They fed themselves in desultory fashion and then drifted around the house without getting engaged in anything. Apparently their electronic games and communications could no longer satisfy. Going out somewhere wasn't an option due to the continuing rainfall and the household's lack of an available vehicle. Spork regretted having come on foot the day before, but had no intention of braving the storm now to retrieve his own ride.

Though the kids didn't seem especially prone to misbehavior, Spork could see that their boredom might lead to problems if allowed to fester all afternoon. He had to think of something. In his own dimly remembered youth, electronic pastimes had not entirely supplanted more primitive ways of spending a rainy afternoon. The present group had never heard of board games and card games, and of course the household wasn't equipped for them, but Spork thought he might invent something along those lines. After a good deal of thought he got an idea for an updated version of an ancient board game, in which the house itself could serve as the board. Possibly the kids could find such a diversion amusing given a chance to help work out its details.

In the recreation room Spork found various hobby-related items including an artist's sketchpad and a paper cutter. He tore out one of the heavy sheets from the sketchpad and used the paper cutter to divide it into twenty-one rectangular pieces of identical size. When appropriately marked, these could serve as playing cards. Spork took them to the kitchen table and began writing the names of rooms on some of them. Riley came in and watched for a moment, then asked what he was doing.

"We're going to play an old-fashioned game!" said Spork with partly feigned enthusiasm. "It will be a new version called Safe Space. I assume your world still has safe spaces, meaning places where people in certain categories can feel safe from oppression because everybody else has to keep away."

"Sure," said Riley, "the schools are full of safe spaces. I hear the colleges are too. After college people just maintain safe spaces in some of the restaurants and clubs and parks where they spend their free time."

"Well, in the game I've got in mind, the players—you three—will be trying to guess which room in this house is a safe space for some category of people. The house happens to have nine rooms, not counting bathrooms, so nine of the cards will represent rooms. Six will represent racial or other ethnic groups, and six will represent sex-related categories. With all the cards face down, we'll draw one room card and one ethnic card and one sexuality card. Then we'll set these aside without looking at them and deal out the remaining cards to the three players. The game will consist of moving around from room to room while you take turns trying to guess whether each room is the safe space described by the hidden cards. For example, suppose I'm Carson and we're in the kitchen and I say: 'The kitchen is a safe space for African American transsexuals.' You will disprove this statement by showing me—but not Hunter—one of these cards if you've got one. If you don't have any, Hunter will show me but not you a card if ze has one. In this way I gain information in hopes of eventually making the correct guess. The turns and showing of cards always proceed in the same order, such as Carson-Riley-Hunter, the order I've just been assuming."

By this time Hunter and Carson had come into the kitchen, so Spork repeated the description as necessary. He had already decided to deviate from the original game by having all the players move together from room to room. They would be obliged to move between turns, at the direction of the person whose turn was coming up, and for simplicity they would only be allowed to move between adjacent rooms. This left the task of selecting racial/ethnic and sex-related categories, which brought some controversy.

"What do you mean by 'sex-related'" asked Carson.

"Well, I was thinking we would include the components of LGBT, plus maybe heterosexual females and something else."

"Those categories don't have much to do with safe spaces," said Hunter. "People don't get harassed for being gay or lesbian anymore."

"Yes they do," said Riley. "Maybe not when they're old, but kids in school and even in college like to put down other kids who're different from themselves."

"At least we shouldn't include bisexuals," rejoined Hunter. "Everyone is bisexual."

"What we're trying to do with these categories," interrupted Spork, "is express what the creators of safe spaces used to call the *intersectionality* of personal characteristics needing protection. For example, gay African Americans might have vulnerabilities differing from those of lesbian African Americans, so these two groups shouldn't be included in the same safe space. If you don't like citing bisexuals, we can eliminate that element. Then we can include both heterosexual females and males, while also splitting up transsexuals by their chosen gender. This will give us six categories."

"You're saying that het males deserve safe spaces?" asked Hunter incredulously.

"Well, over the years there's been so much heartfelt effort to help straight white males manage their guilt that they now have a lot of guilt to manage. This can be manipulated in harmful ways, so such people can benefit from safe spaces whether or not they deserve them. The same might apply to het males in other ethnic groups. Anyway, we're just making up a game. Now then, what about racial and ethnic categories?"

"African American and Hispanic for sure," said Hunter.

"Also Native American and Jewish and Asian," added Riley.

"This leaves one category, which maybe we should reserve for some nationality that's mostly Islamic. Any suggestions?"

"Iraqis," said Carson.

"Fine. Now we just need to prepare the cards and give you a way to make notes. Hunter, take these six cards and write a sex-related category on each one. Riley, you can do the racial/ethnic cards."

Meanwhile Spork took a regular sheet of paper and listed all twenty-one categories down the left-hand side, then used a ruler to divide the remaining space with vertical lines. He made copies of this sheet and passed them out while explaining that players would need to record all the cards they'd seen in order to figure out, by a process of elimination, which cards had been set aside in the solution pile. They could deploy various strategies for record-keeping and formulating guesses and deciding which cards to show, but of course they could also win games just by making lucky guesses.

Spork shuffled the three sets of cards separately and drew one card from each set to go in the solution pile. Then he shuffled the remaining cards together and dealt them out to the players. Waving away possible objections, he arbitrarily said that Carson would go first in the initial game and that play would always proceed in the order currently found around the kitchen table, which was Carson-Riley-Hunter. This meant that Riley would always be the first responder to Carson's guesses, whereas Hunter would be Riley's first responder and Carson would be Hunter's.

"The kitchen is a safe space for het female Iraqis," said Carson after some reflection. Riley showed zirm a card and then led the group into the dining room for zir turn. The game was underway.

"The dining room is a safe space for male transsexual Native Americans," said Riley, who was disabused of this notion by a card from Hunter. Spork had decided to follow the players around for a while to make sure they were playing the game correctly. At first they seemed to be unsure about the note-taking process, with Riley scratching out one or two entire columns of zir sheet and Hunter starting over on a new one, but within a half-dozen turns they had all settled down into systems of one kind or another.

The first game seemed to run on for a long time. Spork noticed several occasions when players managed to get shown cards they'd already seen. But as the game progressed there were more and more times when first responders had no cards to show, and a few turns when nothing got shown. The failure of the latter occasions to end the game indicated that the players had learned to target their guesses by having them include one or two of their own cards.

Finally Carson said the recreation room was a safe space for heterosexual Hispanic males. When nobody had any of these cards, ze exclaimed, "That's it!" Spork turned over the cards in the solution pile to show this was correct. Carson declined to say anything about zir winning methods.

Spork arranged the cards for the second game but then retired to the den with a book. He could hear the group roaming around the house until eventually there was a cry of victory from Hunter. The dining room had turned out to be a safe space for female Native American transsexuals. Hunter initially insisted that zir victory had been a matter of deduction, but under pressure from Riley finally admitted that it had been a lucky guess.

The kids handled the cards themselves for the third game while Spork stayed with his book. After a fairly short time, the players happened to be gathered in the den around Spork's armchair when Carson announced another victory, this time for revealing that they were in a safe space for Jewish lesbians. Out of curiosity Spork asked to see Carson's note sheet and took it out of zir hand before ze could think to refuse. Carson then agreed reluctantly to explain zir notes for the most recent game.

The explanation left Spork impressed. Carson had been recording not only which cards each player was known to possess, but also which ones each player had revealed zirmself to lack by failing to show any as first responder. The latter information had allowed Carson to deduce that lesbians owned the given safe space even though none of zir guesses had ever targeted lesbians. Ze implied that the system served other strategic purposes as well. Carson seemed to be a real smarty.

A fourth game was underway when Spork heard sounds of trouble. There was an argument somewhere in the back of the house, which had moved into the kitchen by the time Spork got there. Carson was complaining tearfully that Hunter had peeked at zir cards. Hunter was emphatically denying this charge, and Riley seemed to be backing zirm up. Spork thought the source of the problem might be a realization by the other two that Carson would be a consistent winner if they played fair.

"I'm tired of this game," said Hunter, with signs of agreement from Riley. "Let's make up something else. I know what: We can play Unsafe Space. One person says something and the others have to guess which specific group of people it would oppress."

"Sounds cool," said Riley. "can you give an example?"

Hunter thought for a minute. "Okay, how about asking the question: 'Which one of you has to wear the burqa?'"

"Gay Iraqis!" said Riley triumphantly.

"But that question would also target lesbian Iraqis," objected Carson. "Any words that would offend more than one group should be inadmissible."

"I agree in general," said Hunter, "but my example is still good. It selects for males because female Iraqis wouldn't be insulted by the idea of wearing a burqa."

"Obviously there's going to be a lot of room for interpretation," mused Riley. "Who'll be the judge of what statements are admissible and what responses are correct?"

"Don't look at me," said Spork. He wasn't comfortable with this turn of events and knew he should go away, but couldn't help being curious about how the new game would turn out. After a moment he retreated to one corner of the kitchen and saw that the kids would be happy to ignore him.

"It's simple," said Hunter. "We've got three people, so for each turn of the game one person can be the verbal oppressor, one can try to identify the oppressed group, and one can be the judge of everything. If the judge says the oppressor's words aren't properly targeted, the oppressor loses. If the words are okay but the identifier doesn't name the correct target group, the identifier loses. If there's a correct identification, nobody loses. We'll rotate around so that each of us gets to play each role with each combination of other people."

"I've got an idea," said Riley. "To keep oppressors from just picking easy targets, we can use the cards to assign them. For each turn the judge shuffles the racial/ethnic cards and draws one, then does the same with the sex-related cards. After looking at the cards ze has drawn, the judge passes them to the oppressor, who must then target the group they identify."

"One more thing," said Hunter. "Merely adding up losses would be kind of boring, so here's a way to make the game more interesting. The other day I was reading a book written a century ago in which the characters played something called strip poker. It wasn't clear what poker was all about, but the important thing was that each time somebody lost, ze had to take off an item of clothing. The game would keep going until someone was completely naked. We could punish losses the same way."

Carson recoiled and opened zir mouth to speak, but then kept quiet. Spork had noticed earlier that Carson hated being left out of anything. Meanwhile Riley greeted the suggestion with enthusiasm.

Hunter nominated zirmself to be the first judge and drew two cards from the relevant piles. Ze looked at them and then passed them along to Riley, who was to be the first oppressor. Riley thought for a minute and then said, "I bet your hair made beautiful cornrows back when you were female."

"African American male transsexual," said Carson immediately.

"Hey, I was still deciding whether that statement was admissible," objected Hunter. "Both male and female African Americans sometimes wear their hair in cornrows."

"But my statement makes clear which gender would have been wearing the cornrows in this case. Notice the insult involved in addressing the target as a former female rather than as a male in a former female body."

"Okay, that's oppressive, but where's the insult in linking a certain kind of hairstyle to people with a certain kind of hair?"

"It's a *microaggression*," answered Riley. "That's a lot of what college kids talk about when defending the need for safe spaces. Any reference to a racial or sexual characteristic, no matter how subtle, can be considered a microaggression if not spoken by someone having that characteristic. In fact, we should make it a rule of Unsafe Space that references just have to be identifiable, whether or not they're offensive in any way an outsider can imagine."

After some discussion, the group adopted this rule and determined that there had been no loser in the first round. The next round featured Carson as judge, Hunter as oppressor, and Riley as identifier. Hunter had to target heterosexual male Asians, and even with much cogitation ze couldn't come up with a way to do it. "Off with zir shirt," said Riley.

Only at this point did Spork think about the limitations of the game. Because the kids were barefooted and dressed for summer weather, they were probably wearing only three or four items of clothing apiece. In no time they would be mostly if not completely naked. Spork realized he would find this situation awkward, although it might clear up a couple of questions about the kids' genders, so he went back to his book in the den.

Various snatches of conversation came from the kitchen. At one point there was a loud argument about a reference to an itchy scalp, which Riley insisted was sufficient to target a Native American. Apparently someone lost zir pants on this interchange.

Then a few minutes later Spork could hear chairs overturning and the kitchen table sliding across the floor, accompanied by shrill sounds of protest. He looked in to find Hunter and Riley finishing the job of undressing Carson. Then Hunter, who was already naked, attacked Riley's undergarment and managed to get it off. Carson had already fled somewhere in the back of the house, and the other two disappeared in that direction.

There was a long moment of silence. Then came a stampede down the hallway and into the living room. Carson was being chased by Riley, who was swinging one of the big overstuffed pillows from Morgan's bedroom, and Hunter was pursuing Riley with a similar pillow. Carson curled up on the living room floor and took a quick pounding, but then Hunter's assault on Riley demanded retaliatory attention. Soon Hunter and Riley got wrapped up in attempts to immobilize each other's pillows, causing them to fall in a heap on the sofa where Spork had slept the night before.

Then they were having sex. Spork may have blinked when this started; he just knew it wasn't happening one moment and the next moment it definitely was. Carson was standing next to the sofa looking left-out when ze was pulled into the action as well. The resulting assemblage was unique in Spork's lengthy but not wide-ranging experience. Even if they were ready, they couldn't make many babies that way, thought Spork.

Suddenly the front door opened and Morgan walked in, a bit earlier than expected. On entering the living room she pointedly asked, "What are my pillows doing on the floor?" Spork hastily said they had been part of a brief game that didn't damage anything. "Well, don't mess up the sofa," she told the kids over her shoulder while heading toward her bedroom with the pillows and her overnight bag.

In leisurely fashion the kids untangled themselves and wandered into the kitchen to reclaim their clothes. They were dressed by the time Morgan came back. She exchanged some pleasantries with Hunter and Carson, whom she barely knew, and told them to gather their belongings because she would be taking them home. Meanwhile Spork collected his own things from the den and noticed that the rain had stopped outside.

When Hunter and Carson were ready to go, Morgan turned to Spork as if noticing him for the first time. "Oh, thanks for looking after the children. Would you like me to drop you off at your house?"

"No, that's okay," said Spork. "I'd rather walk."

5

NATURE'S BOUNTY

❝ Thank you, thank you. I'll be saying a few words tonight on a subject very different from those addressed by other speakers at this conference. In fact it's not a topic you'd ever expect to hear about at a Chamber of Commerce proceeding. We are generally known for opposing government interference in private enterprise. As a matter of principle we spend a great deal of time and effort fighting intrusive government regulations. Yet tonight I'm here to celebrate the hundred-year anniversary of a federal regulatory program. It's a program that our predecessors in the business community fought tooth and nail. But they were wrong. They had no idea what benefits could accrue from such an initiative.

"I'm talking about the Endangered Species Act of 1973. A hundred years ago, almost to the day, this Act was signed into law to prevent the extinction of imperiled plant and animal life and to support the recovery of such populations. This would be achieved mainly by prohibiting or limiting the 'taking' of individual specimens—which basically meant harming them in any way—and by protecting the ecosystems upon which they depended. The latter goal would be achieved by designating so-called critical habitat for a species and limiting activities in this area as needed for its recovery. I won't bore you with details about how the program has worked, how various forces once tried to undermine it, and how its operation has been consistently supported by the courts. Instead I'll just tell a few stories that illustrate the amazing and unforeseen benefits of the Endangered Species Act.

"One of the best outcomes occurred early on. In 1973, the same year the Act was passed, biologists looking for ways to stop a TVA dam project on the Little Tennessee River discovered a tiny fish living only in a section of that river slated for inundation. Work on the dam was then halted to protect the given fish, known as a snail darter, in an action ultimately affirmed by the Supreme Court. The dam project was probably a poor choice to begin with, but the structure was virtually complete when construction stopped, yielding great political pressure to let it serve its purpose of power generation at little further expense. Thus in a never-repeated move Congress granted the project a special exception from the Endangered Species Act. But all was not lost for the snail darter. Before its habitat in the Little Tennessee was flooded, specimens of the snail darter were relocated to a nearby river, where the species thrived to such an extent that it was removed from the endangered species list in five years.

"The climax of the story came fifty years later. The focus of scientific attention on the snail darter led to a discovery that this otherwise defenseless little perch was protected by a special secretion on its scales that repulsed potential predators. The active ingredient in this secretion was synthesized in a laboratory and turned out to be highly amenable to mass production. Thus was born the universally popular shark repellant known as JawsAway. All the major manufacturers of suntan lotion and sunblock began to include JawsAway in their products as a bonus feature, with the result that shark attacks on our shores have been drastically reduced.

"Even though other parties are responsible for implementing the Endangered Species Act, the Environmental Protection Agency has been given the job of quantifying benefits from this source due to that agency's special knack for pinpoint estimation of environmentally related human impacts. The EPA's calculations in this case have had to allow for the vast increase in shark attacks that would have occurred without JawsAway due to the proliferation of sharks enjoying endangered-species protection. The bottom line is that over the past forty-five years, the survival of the snail darter—an indirect but indisputable consequence of the Endangered Species Act—has saved 2,250 U.S. residents from fatal shark attacks and tens of thousands more from shark-related injuries.

"Another application of the Endangered Species Act resembled the case of the snail darter in that the species in question was suddenly discovered in the 1970s by opponents of an unpopular dam project. Unlike the snail darter, the given species was previously known but thought to be extinct, and its presence ultimately defeated the dam project that threatened it. Another difference was that the organism in question was not an animal but a plant, a thirty-inch 'fugitive species' known as the Furbish lousewort.

"The Furbish lousewort lived only on steep north-facing and west-facing riverbanks, namely those along a 140-mile stretch of the St. John River in Maine and New Brunswick. It required shading by adjacent vegetation and needed particular kinds of disturbance by the river—flooding and ice-scouring, but not soil dumping or denudation—to propagate itself. After several years of existence it would send up a 'single, slightly hairy and reddish' stem bearing a cluster of small yellow flowers.

"After the cancellation of the dam project in 1986, the Furbish lousewort lived on in obscurity for several decades until rumors spread among counterculture communities along the St. John River that lousewort flowers had wondrous psychoactive properties. The scientific establishment took notice and conducted experiments in which young subjects were set to work snorting lousewort blossoms under laboratory conditions. These tests showed that essence of lousewort was an extremely powerful antidepressant with no adverse side effects. Further testing isolated the responsible agent, a compound that selectively stimulated dopamine neurons in the dorsal raphe nucleus of the brain. No way was ever found to obtain a synthetic version of this compound, but on the upside, an agricultural conglomerate developed methods of cultivating the Furbish lousewort by simulating its favored riverine conditions. In no time commercial lousewort farms swept across the St. John valley and transformed the economy of northern Maine.

"The resulting product was especially effective in preventing suicide. Something about the lousewort's determination to survive under brutal conditions gave its chemistry the power to make people buck up and carry on. Although aggressive pricing by the patent-holding pharmaceutical company has limited the population able to afford lousewort therapy, the EPA has estimated that 25,000 lives have been saved so far as a lousewort-related benefit of the Endangered Species Act.

"The story of the gray wolf illustrates that a threat of extinction, as defined by the Endangered Species Act and its implementers, doesn't really mean that an organism might cease to exist. It means that a species might cease to occupy some portion of its historical range. Throughout the present century there have been about fifteen thousand gray wolves in the U.S., the majority living in Alaska without federal protection. About two thousand gray wolves occupy the northern Rocky Mountains, and another four thousand are found in the western Great Lakes states, primarily Minnesota. Both of the latter populations enjoy endangered-species protection under court order. The Rocky Mountain wolves serve to control the elk population, notably in Yellowstone national Park, but the Minnesota wolves are protected only because they were always present before humanity barged in.

"The wisdom of enduring greater and greater wolf-related conflicts in Minnesota was brought home in mid-century by a scientific discovery. It was found that proximity to civilization had caused Minnesota wolves to develop a unique gastric enzyme to facilitate the digestion of farm animals and household pets. Artificially synthesized versions of this enzyme proved to be strikingly effective at arresting stomach and colorectal cancers in human subjects. This led to a commercially available cancer drug, marketed under the name Lupusol, which has already saved an EPA-certified 225,000 lives.

"The western U.S. has three subspecies of spotted owls, of which the Mexican and northern subspecies are listed under the Endangered Species Act. Early in this century there were an estimated 2,106 Mexican spotted owls in the U.S., widely scattered across Arizona, New Mexico, west Texas, and southern Utah and Colorado. At that time a critical habitat totaling 8,600,000 acres was established for the protection of this subspecies. The designated habitat slightly exceeded the area of New Jersey plus Connecticut and worked out to more than 4,000 acres per Mexican spotted owl.

"In 2040 a group of scientists working at the Mexican Spotted Owl Rescue Mission became interested in the ability of this species to come smiling through the vicious dust storms that plagued the southwestern deserts as a result of global warming. To make a long story short, the given investigators discovered a suite of pituitary hormones that if introduced into humans would greatly increase their resistance to airborne particulates. Throughout the present century the EPA has steadfastly maintained that air pollution in the form of particulate matter kills 160,000 Americans per year. Administering the given hormones to persons at pulmonary risk could easily reduce this death toll by half. Thus, spotted-owl therapy could already have saved 2,400,000 lives.

"But this saving hasn't been achieved, even in part, because scientists have never succeeded in developing synthetic versions of the chemicals in question. Sacrificing live owls—each with hormones potent enough to save thousands of people—hasn't been possible because takings of this animal are prohibited by the Endangered Species Act.

"A conservationist once said of the snail darter that it: 'arrived…the hard way, the Darwinian way, through millions of years of random variation and natural selection, reaching its culmination in a small homely animal resembling a sculpin, something far more than a net asset in potential utility.' We wouldn't presume to disagree, but the same could be said of all species that ever existed on earth, over ninety percent of which are now extinct. What matters from a Chamber of Commerce perspective is the human payoff, and I'm happy to report that except for the spotted-owl impasse, the Endangered Species Act has delivered."

6

FAITH

"What you're calling my religious quest is all your fault, you know."

"Why do you say that?"

"You insisted on taking me to church when I was little. You made me go to Sunday school, and even had me enrolled in confirmation classes before I managed to make my escape. So I got filled with propaganda—which you pretty much supported—before I was old enough to think for myself. My mother would never have done that to me."

"No, she wouldn't have, but she probably knew I would."

"I'm not complaining in general. You've been wonderful, Nana, and I owe you more than I could possibly say. But how was all that religious indoctrination supposed to be good for me?"

"I thought that Christianity was... had a lot to offer. I still do. And I felt that denying you religious training might cost you something besides Christianity. Children can acquire a capacity for religious faith much more readily than adults, and this is a precious gift no matter what one eventually does with it. I didn't take your mother to church or teach her about such matters because her father, the grandfather you never knew, detested organized religion. I've always regretted this."

"Whether or not a capacity for faith is a gift, it's certainly a burden. Children acquire it while being taught that the most basic questions about our existence—things that rational people consider unknowable—all have answers. This idea persists even after the church's other teachings are rejected, so the child of faith is driven to find substitute answers. That's apparently the origin of my quest. Based on what little we hear from her, my mother's freedom from this burden has left her better off."

"I don't think she's better off. She's no less driven than you are; she just looks for meaning in different places. Her quest focuses partly on her work, but mostly on relationships—romance, love, sex, so forth. She has sacrificed a great deal for this sort of thing, and her record suggests that she has less chance than you do of ever finding peace. Some of her wandering can be traced to her history of uneasy relations with her father, but I can't help thinking her life would have turned out better if I'd given her more structure early on. Of course, if that were true she might not have left you for me to raise after your father left, so I can't say I'm sorry. But back to your quest, you talk as if rejecting everything you learned in church was an absolute necessity. Why?"

"Nana, by the time I grew up in the first quarter of this century, Christianity had been declining for decades and was almost a spent force. The reasons can be summarized by saying that Christianity was—and still is, to the extent that it survives—on the wrong side of history."

"I didn't know history had sides."

"Sure. They exist because history has a direction of flow. Anything that goes with the flow is on the right side of history, and anything that resists is on the wrong side. Christianity is wrong for all sorts of reasons, but most of them revolve around the fact that it's patriarchal."

"Patriarchal?"

"The monotheistic religions have always been patriarchal. When people had to have a single, all-powerful god, it—he—was inevitably going to be male. No other outcome was possible given our state of evolution when the major religions were born. And any religion centering upon a male godhead was naturally going to be authoritarian. So we got commandments and punishments, good and evil, heaven and hell, the whole Biblical catastrophe."

"I can't say your complaint isn't valid for the Old Testament, which can reasonably be called authoritarian. But Christianity isn't about the Old Testament; it's about things that happened and got recorded later. Jesus didn't speak with overtones of patriarchal authority. His teachings about love, humility, turning the other cheek, doing unto others, and so on were practically feminine in emphasis."

"You're right, and that's the great irony of Christianity. The message of love and mercy got lost as the church organized itself into a political force and an instrument of social control."

"What about the churches we attended when you were little? Their preachers weren't fundamentalists who insisted on interpreting the whole Bible as literal truth, or fire-and-brimstone types who tried to scare everybody into being good."

"No, you made sure that our preachers weren't Bible-thumpers. They were pretty mellow as a rule. But the same didn't go for Sunday-school teachers and all the other people leaning on me. Most of them truly believed in heaven and hell and the possibility of eternal damnation. And my argument about the basic nature of Christianity has been confirmed by what's happened to the faith since I grew up. The mellow preachers have all gone, their churches closed due to lack of interest. Monotheism can't run on sweetness and light. An all-powerful deity makes no sense unless the power is used for something, and in today's atmosphere of skepticism toward authority, most people can't buy the idea that godly power exists to reward or punish them in the afterlife."

"Christianity has been declining, I'll grant you, but there are still lots of active denominations."

"Look at what's left. On one hand there's a fundamentalist rump, a hard-core residual passing along the same old doctrines to fewer and fewer people. On the other hand there are denominations that shift the goals of piety from the hereafter to the here-and-now. If you say your prayers just right, Jesus will make you rich. This spin on the faith has appeal in certain quarters but is hardly what could be called Christianity."

"What about all the people trying to lead Christian lives? The faith involves a demanding moral code as well as a set of beliefs. I'm still surrounded by people who try—admittedly with varying degrees of success— to live according to that code."

"Yes, but if you'll pardon my saying so, these are undoubtedly old folks like you. Allegiance to Christian morality has essentially died out among younger people. There's a reason for this over and above the doctrinal misalignment I've mentioned. It is that Christian teaching sets an impossible standard of behavior. No amount of self-sacrifice and service to others can be good enough. This fact along with original sin accounts for the continual need to apologize and beg forgiveness. At least Islam is an achievable practice. Pray five times a day, fast during Ramadan, make the haj, follow other clear-cut rules and you're in. But Christianity never lets you off the hook."

"It makes me sad to hear you talk this way. God is love; that's the message of Christianity. Why can't its practice keep this message but otherwise change along with the times? Why can't your generation set aside the Old Testament, if it's so irrevocably patriarchal, and simply declare that the Christian deity is female? You've already admitted that the teachings of Jesus, if not the Jesus figure per se, would be consistent with this."

"Nana, it's too late. Christianity followed a traditional path, with authoritarian tendencies outweighing its good works, for too long to permit any sort of latter-day reformation. The barriers to this include all the hard-to-swallow elements of Christian dogma: the virgin birth, the Biblical miracles, the three-in-one godhead, the resurrected bodies, the practice of cannibalism by transubstantiation. There's also the fact that Christian observances are disconnected from daily life, unlike those of what have become its rival faiths. If you like, I can tell you about the religions that are now ascendant and explain why they're suited to modern needs."

"I'm mostly interested in your needs, but yes, fill me in on what's happened in the world of religion since I lost touch."

"As you probably know, my main focus over the past dozen years has been Wicca, so we may as well start there. Wicca originated in England around the middle of the last century and was initially just called witchcraft. It invoked purportedly ancient deities and incorporated a variety of pagan beliefs and practices.

Observers referenced it variously as a magico-religion and a form of nature worship. Early forms of Wicca were mostly duotheistic, with a Moon Goddess representing the female principle and a Horned God representing the male. Later versions were pantheistic or polytheistic or monotheistic, with the divinity in the last case being female or genderless. Some Wiccans were atheists who saw the deities just as metaphorical archetypes or thoughtforms.

"Wicca quickly became so diverse that it was most easily describable in terms of what it wasn't, namely Christianity. This divergence didn't go so far as devil-worship, but involved basic aspects of Wicca such as the facts that it lacked any central authority like the Bible; that its deity or deities were immanent, often dwelling in nature, rather than remote; that its deities could affect human lives but didn't exist to pass judgment on them; that belief in an afterlife wasn't central to Wicca; that there was no Wiccan heaven or hell; and that Wicca had no fixed moral guidelines other than an admonition to avoid harming other people.

"By turn of the century in the U.S., Wiccan beliefs and practices had become substantially aligned with progressive politics. Two overriding emphases were feminism and protection of the environment, both of which suffused the faith in multiple ways. Another progressive element was celebration of sexual expression in all its forms. Then over the course of this century the feminist ascendency in U.S. society at large allowed a relative shift of attention toward nature and its spiritual ramifications. Accompanying this shift was a split in Wiccan practice involving types of religious observances and their degree of integration into daily life.

"On one hand we now have what could be called the ritual Wiccans. These are persons whose practice of the faith is mainly limited to periodic ceremonies having an exclusively religious focus. The celebrants meet in groups, or covens, at eight seasonal festivals collectively called the Wheel of the Year. There they form sacred circles and cast spells and perform other types of magic, accompanied by music, dance, song and various forms of pageantry. Although godly intervention is sometimes an objective, the rituals are intended mainly to induce religious experience in the participants. The Wiccans in question value the rituals for their own sake and don't make special efforts to align the rest of their lives with the faith.

"Today's other Wiccans have brought forward their love and perhaps worship of nature into an ongoing preoccupation. This reflects a tendency of all the leading modern faiths to integrate religious observances into daily life. Incidentally, I should note that many Wiccans don't call their faith a religion—preferring some term like 'spirituality'—and the same applies to the other cases I'll be mentioning. But I have to agree with whoever it was who said that if something talks like a religion and acts like a religion, then it must be a religion.'"

"Excuse me, but don't you think a religion has to involve worshipping some kind of deity?"

"Not necessarily. A very old and widespread Asian religion, which has been factored into one of the modern faiths, is a system of naturalistic morality that doesn't focus on any divinity at all. There's probably need for a supernatural element of some kind, but what really matters is having a belief system that creates meaning for its adherents and gives them opportunities for personal affirmation. Throw in some observances to be offered on a regular basis, with an element of sacrifice and at least a little fervor, and you've got yourself a religion.

"Back to the nature-oriented Wiccans, there's been a split between two groups that are closely associated but distinguishable on the basis of their observances. What we can call the earth Wiccans are preoccupied if not obsessed with saving the environment. For them, chaining one's self to a tree or going off the grid or recycling one's garbage is essentially a religious act. Some of these practitioners are earth-worshippers serving a pantheistic deity, while others are simply addressing secular concerns about environmental degradation, but either way both the driver and the product consist of religious piety.

"The other group consists of animal-loving Wiccans. These practitioners obviously share the same concerns as earth Wiccans, since the survival and health of animal species depend on the overall condition of the biosphere, but their observances are more specifically animal-focused. These can range from animal-sighting expeditions and support for wildlife programs down to petting one's cat. Outright animal-worship is not unknown. Offsetting the relatively narrow range of observances in this case is the fact that animals are emotionally engaging. Among other things this makes them readily substitutable for expensive and environmentally damaging children."

"Where has your practice of Wicca placed you among these groups?"

"For the most part I've been a ritual Wiccan. I always found the seasonal gatherings, or Sabbats, to be quite moving in a general sort of way and also a lot of fun. Not coincidentally, I joined one of the last covens to have a strongly feminist emphasis. Smashing patriarchy was a holy mission I could really get behind. But over time my sisters of the Craft faced the fact that patriarchy was a dead horse and shifted their attention to environmental concerns. I don't happen to be a pantheist, or any other sort of theist for that matter. So although I care as much about the planet and its denizens as anybody, I can't acquire the sort of religiosity about nature that most other Wiccans possess. This has left me at loose ends and restarted what you call my religious quest."

"So your soul is still up for grabs? I'll have to tell my preacher about that. Sorry, just kidding."

"I haven't been terribly attracted by either of the other modern religions, but they may have features I haven't explored yet. In any case I'll tell you about them. They both surpass nature-oriented Wicca in suffusing daily life with religious significance, and in fact their practice is built around the fulfillment of daily needs. I like their feminist associations, in that they reflect traditionally female interests and sensibilities, but not their tendency to verge into self-worship.

"One of these new religions—I'll explain its name in a minute—is based on the burgeoning obsession with food and bodily nourishment. Since I seem to be exempt, I find myself referring to this obsession as food faddism. It's a bit ironic that as dietary options have continued to expand, people have gotten more and more restrictive about what they eat. Some of the restrictions are philosophically based, most notably the avoidance of meat and other animal products. Practitioners commonly cite health benefits, but the fact that most vegetarians and vegans won't eat a single bite of the proscribed victuals would suggest that theirs is a religious choice. Other restrictions are linked more directly to health concerns, supported in widely varying degrees by medical science. Without judging the overall value of these limitations, I can't help noticing that as the experts call for more and more dietary taboos to address specific medical conditions, more and more people are finding themselves afflicted with the very same conditions. At any rate, the need to worry over food contents and compensate for forbidden foodstuffs in fulfilling nutritional requirements can make food faddism very time-consuming, so it's ideal as a basis for the modern sort of religious observance.

"This preoccupation has been grafted onto the ancient Asian religion I mentioned a few minutes ago.

The advantages of this religion for today's religious shoppers include its lack of authority figures, its casual attitude toward rules and transgressions, and its concept of diffuse and undemanding love. It teaches that craving and other forms of willfulness are the source of suffering and entrapment in an endless cycle of rebirth. By looking inward to find wisdom, the practitioner can escape this cycle and attain a state of absolute bliss called nirvana. The worst that can happen is that an absence of wisdom and compassion can lead to rebirth as a lower faunal type.

"The union of this spiritual framework with food orientation has yielded the modern religion known as Foodhism. The unifying theme is self-absorption. Foodhism is a logical extension of our ever more popular self-help culture. The dedicated Foodhist looks inward for wisdom, but need only look as far as zir own digestive system. The inherited admonition against craving has been modified to cover only craving for improper foodstuffs. Nirvana is the self-admiration acquired by contemplating one's own wellbeing. The observances that occupy and elevate Foodhist attention include all aspects of analyzing, acquiring, preparing and ingesting holy meals."

"Somehow I can tell you're less than thrilled by this option."

"To be honest, Nana, what really matter to me are observances. Those offered by Foodhism lack drama, and in general they're too solitary and solipsistic. I can't quite get into worshipping my own body. The same criticisms largely apply to the last religion I'm going to mention, but at least it addresses the body in a more imaginative way.

"The preoccupation that led to the development of this religion was the mania for physical culture. Exercise was potentially ideal as a basis for religious observances because it could consume any time and resources available; because training regimes could be arbitrarily stringent; and because such activity invited ritual self-sacrifice. An obstacle to be overcome, however, was that birth-males were bigger and stronger than birth-females, and exercise on both parts tended to maintain if not accentuate this difference. Excessive male musculature had always been associated with oppression and violence, besides which its existence was widely regarded as an offense against gender equality. So the packaging of religiosity in this case had to focus on the *right* sort of physical culture. Fortunately, an ancient tradition filled this need by offering an elaborate exercise regimen based on the premise that muscles should be stretched rather than used.

"The religion most closely associated with this tradition involved many gods and goddesses, possibly one for every purpose, creating a spiritual nexus that the Western mind found inscrutable. For the modern participant this was as good as having no deities at all. Meanwhile the exercise regimen in question had meditative and spiritual dimensions that Westerners found useful for relieving stress and suppressing pesky mental activity. Advanced practitioners attained godlike levels of flexibility, letting them assume postures that defied ordinary human physiology, mostly for the sake of defying ordinary human physiology. The aspect of greatest interest to Westerners was that practitioners tended to be very thin. Whether this was because the regimen discouraged eating or because its followers favored roughage over protein, thinness was an outcome that modern observers could recognize as both holy and fashionable.

"Hence we have Thinduism. Recently I've given some thought to becoming a Thindu. The ritual exercise sessions have a nice communal aspect, and Thinduism deals more elaborately than Foodhism with mind-body connections. I never would have thought so much attention could be paid to the act of breathing. On the other hand, Thinduism puts no more emphasis than Foodhism on good works and other forms of outreach. Maybe I'm a hollow sort of person, but I just can't convince myself that all essential truth can be extracted from my own corporeal and maybe spiritual being."

"You haven't said anything about Islam."

"That's because it's a retrograde phallocentric practice not worth mentioning."

"But I've read somewhere that Islam is the country's fastest-growing religion. The faiths you mention have only increased at the expense of Christianity. The non-Islamic population as a whole is declining. In fact its rate of decline has gotten quite significant."

"This isn't due to conversion among faiths. The reason is that Muslim fertility is two to three times as high as everybody else's, because Islamic culture forces women to have babies."

"Why does the fertility of other groups have to be so low?"

"Most men still avoid sharing fully in the domestic responsibilities created by children. If this weren't the case, progressive women would be happy to bear more of them."

"You're telling men to be just like women. Which most of them can't, because they lack the necessary resources, so they tend to react by avoiding commitment and behaving in ways you call sexist. Anyway, I have to ask how much truth a religion can offer if it can't even see to its own survival."

"Nana, your problem is that you still believe in a god. If there's no deity to worry about the future of a religion, or the future of humanity in general, I feel no need to worry either."

"Very well. Maybe when you're older."

7

REPLACEMENT

The front door opened to reveal an unexpected but not altogether surprising face.

"Simon! What are you doing home?"

"Hello, Mr. Aiken. I'm on spring break."

"Is the Senator here yet? He called me this afternoon and said he'd be home by six. There are some things he wants to discuss before tomorrow."

"Come in, come in. Dad called here a minute ago and said he'd be late due a problem with his flight. I'm supposed to make you comfortable and not let you get away."

"I'll stay if you'll agree to call me Ralph. The 'mister' business reminds me of my age, which has become a sensitive issue now that I've been identified as the oldest Senate staffer on the Hill. It's ironic that I'm working for the youngest Senator in our party. Of course, your Dad occupies this position only because we Contrarians are a dying breed."

Simon escorted Ralph Aiken to a seat in the living room and brought him a drink, then sat down nearby.

"Say, what's the story with the 'self-replacement' bill that's got the Senate in such a tizzy? Dad never tells me anything."

"He probably doesn't think you're interested, and maybe there's some resentment of the fact that you went into engineering rather than following in his political footsteps."

"Could be. I don't regret my choice, which admittedly had an element of teenage rebellion. But after pointedly refusing to learn anything about government, I now find myself getting curious. So why is this current bill such a big deal?"

"It's a big deal for two reasons: because it addresses an important issue that's been avoided up till now, and because it has created—or perhaps just brought to the surface—an unprecedented split among the Femocrats."

"Femocrats?"

"That's an old name for Progressives reflecting their pro-female, politically correct tilt. I still like using it, along with referring to our party as Contrarians rather than Conservatives in acknowledgement of our marginal status."

"How did favoring women yield such dominance, when the country had nearly as many male voters as females?"

"My reference to Femocrats as pro-female is a bit misleading since the posture in question goes way beyond gender-specific issues. There are traditionally male and female ways of looking at things, and what the Femocrats do is favor female-associated values over their male counterparts across the board, which is the essence of political correctness. Anyway, what happened about a half-century ago was that a tipping point was reached at which female commitment to political correctness made it too costly for many men to oppose. Pressure from wives, friends, work associates and so forth created such difficulties for nonconforming males that the more agreeable ones chose to switch rather than fight. This put the Femocrats in charge of what has been—at least until now—a monolithic and unassailable orthodoxy.

"Oh, I should mention the role played by the economy. The Conservatives had inherited from their political predecessors a commitment to small government, but there was no small-government solution to rising income inequality and losses of mid-level jobs. Only the wage subsidy program could address these concerns, and only the Femocrats were ideologically prepared to implement such a system. Consequently the Contrarians lost a great deal of male support, which they've remained too hidebound to win back. As you can tell, I'm not very conservative on economic issues, though it's best not to remind your father of this."

"So what about the present situation?"

"Okay, what's being called the self-replacement bill is a simple answer, or partial answer, to a complex problem. The problem is that the U.S. fertility rate—the average number of lifetime births per woman—has been declining more or less continually for ninety years, since the first decade of this century, and there's no prospect of a turnaround. We Contrarians have plenty to say about the causes of this trend, but I won't get into that. What matters is that the fertility rate is now just three-fourths of the level necessary to sustain an isolated population. We can rely on immigration to fill the gap, but with native births so low, stabilizing the population at any level above zero will require immigrants and their descendants to constitute a rapidly increasing share of the populace. Femocrats say we won't be able to assimilate such immigrant flows fast enough to avoid an erosion of our culture. Their real concern, of course, is erosion of their own political power.

"Other than boosting life expectancy, there are two ways of raising a country's rate of natural increase. One is getting women to have more babies. The other is increasing the share of women in the total population. Do the math: If women are bearing children at three-fourths of what would be the replacement rate for a gender-equal population, they will fully sustain a population in which females outnumber males two-to-one. The proposed self-replacement bill would combine both approaches. It would involve making cash payments to the mothers and other primary custodians of female children in every year through age twenty-one. This would induce women to bear more children and to substitute female for male births. Many details remain to be worked out, such as whether the payments would extend to all female offspring or just first-born females, but that's the basic idea."

"Surely this is something that Progressives— or Femocrats as you call them—would favor and Conservatives would oppose. What aspect of the bill could be a point of contention among Femocrats?"

"Their disagreement is all about ideology. Unlike what I was just saying about political correctness and Femocratic approaches in general, the schism is specifically gender-related. It may have existed for a long time in latent form. It now involves an open division of Femocrats into two camps, the idealists and the pragmatists. What divides them is that for the idealists, gender doesn't exist. They consider it dead, finished, vanquished in concept if not in reality. They can't even speak the word, and they write it in the manner of something obscene, with asterisks in place of the 'en.' Hence they are adamantly opposed to any social action that makes explicit reference to gender. The pragmatists agree that gender shouldn't be an operative principle in any other context, but are willing to acknowledge it as a reproductive fact.

"The one point on which Contrarians and both groups of Femocrats all agree is that low fertility has something to do with the behavioral impacts of male psychology. Successive Femocratic regimes have tried to solve the male problem—whatever it is—by myriad actions to reward traditionally female behavior and punish what's considered toxic maleness. The pragmatic Femocrats now concede that these efforts to make men just like women will never be fully successful. But the idealists refuse to admit defeat. They insist that society should redouble its efforts to eliminate manhood rather than working around it for the sake of demographic stability. Men will finish changing into women simply because they must.

"The self-replacement bill—so called because it would reward each woman who replaces herself and her reproductive potential in the population—may or may not represent an historic watershed. It could turn out to be momentous if the Femocratic schism evoked by the bill persists as an ongoing factor. For years we Contrarians have been so outnumbered that our influence is asymptotically zero. But all of a sudden we seem to hold the fate of the self-replacement bill, and a continuation of the Femocratic split might give us some long-term leverage. I've heard a lot of talk about possible ways to make strategic use of the present situation."

At this point Senator Frank Busby entered the house and came into the room. After greetings were exchanged, the three men went into the kitchen so Busby could fix himself a sandwich, then returned to the living room.

"Mind if I sit in?" Simon asked his father.

"Not at all, if you're interested. We won't be discussing any state secrets."

"Frank, I was just telling Simon about the self-replacement bill and had gotten to the governing party's division on this issue between its idealist and pragmatist wings."

"Oh yes, some of my colleagues are so excited to see the Progressives fight among themselves that they're imagining all sorts of benefits for us down the road. But I'm pretty sure this is an isolated situation. We may play a decisive role in killing the self-replacement bill, but after this moment of glory the Conservative Party will fall back into its usual state of impotence.

"I don't see anything we can do to prolong the Progressive division, and furthermore I don't think the two Progressive camps are as evenly balanced as the self-replacement battle would suggest. Don't forget that the Progressive Party has a lot of male supporters and quite a few male Senators. These traitors to their gender will accept and embrace all sorts of political correctness, but a measure that explicitly seeks to reduce the country's male presence is going too far. So they're joining with the idealists in opposition to the self-replacement bill even though most of them don't belong in that camp. After this fight is over the pragmatists will remain ascendant and thus fully in charge of picking the flesh off our bones.

"It's impossible to overstate how badly we'd be hurt if the self-replacement bill got passed. Men wouldn't go extinct, but Conservative legislators would. Our party now has just twenty senators, not one of whom was elected with more than fifty-five percent of the vote. Given the prevailing party affiliations by gender, a ten-percent shift in each state's voting population from male to female could wipe us all out. How can we benefit from a split among Progressives if we don't have anyone in office to exploit it?"

"Well, I've checked around on the Hill as you asked, and there are a few Conservative senators who think that supporting rather than rejecting the self-replacement bill might gain us something down the road. I don't buy any of their arguments for this kind of strategic voting, because I agree with you that there's nothing we can do to affect the future power relationships within the Progressive Party. But there are two somewhat different ideas that you might want to consider.

"Senator Danforth's legislative director has told me that Danforth would like to see us use our pivotal position to force a change in the self-replacement bill rather than simply voting it up or down. The change would involve control of immigration. As you know, the Conservative Party is picking up a good deal of support from this source because immigrants tend to come from traditional societies wherein males are accustomed to feeling—and are allowed to feel—like men. Thus a continuation of recent trends would cause the Conservative share of voters to level off in the near future and then start to rise. What the Progressives want to do, though they don't talk about this, is reduce the flow of immigration to a low level with the self-replacement policy in effect. Under such a plan the nation's population would stabilize eventually, but since the demographic impacts of self-replacement would take a long time to materialize, the population would decline a lot before reaching an equilibrium. This is the outcome that Danforth's proposal would forestall. He would offer the Progressives a deal in which they could have their self-replacement bill in exchange for allowing enough immigration to hold the nation's population at its present level. Various arguments could be adduced for this, such as maintaining support for national defense and old-age entitlements."

"Two questions. First, could the volume of immigration be controlled legislatively? Up to now it's always been governed by administrative fiat. And second, by creating a high-population scenario with a long-term tilt toward females, would Danforth's deal really leave us better off than we'd be otherwise?"

"Members of Danforth's staff have been working on the first question and think the answer is positive. The volume of immigration has never been addressed legislatively because Progressives are happy with administrative control and Conservatives have never had any chance of pushing through a bill that would take this away. Our present leverage will give us that chance. Danforth's people don't see any problems with writing immigration control into the self-replacement bill, and they even think we can include provisions such as requiring female immigrants not to exceed males.

"The second question is complicated. Danforth's people have looked at a lot of scenarios and time frames.

They point out that the proposed deal will mandate a big increase in immigration, to halt the nation's recent population decline, and assume that in the absence of a deal the Progressives would reduce immigration substantially. They assume that immigrants and their descendants will continue to be slow in converging with the native population in reproductive and political behavior. And they don't expect the self-replacement policy to have a whole lot of demographic impact, based on the failure of birth-rewarding programs in other countries to raise fertility rates significantly. Their bottom line is that for several hundred years, the country will have a larger share of Conservative voters with Danforth's deal than without it. Our male population will be higher in absolute terms, though perhaps not in relative terms."

"What happens after several hundred years?"

"Depending on the outcome of the self-replacement policy, the population could feminize enough to erase these advantages. But we're talking about such a long passage of time that there could be all sorts of unforeseen developments in the interim.

"Something I should mention is that one of the trends sought by the self-replacement bill is already underway without it. In recent years more and more women have been selecting for female children when they decide to give birth. Those willing to explain have almost invariably said that males are too troublesome to raise. Presumably this has something to do with the absence of adult males in over half of all child-rearing households. The upshot is that women of child-bearing age have started to outnumber males in the same age bracket. Simon, when I said that the U.S. fertility rate was down to three-fourths of replacement level, this referred to replacement-level reproduction with the currently skewed gender mix. We're actually below seventy percent of what would be replacement level if there were as many males as females. At any rate, whether this spontaneous trend has any bearing on the likely impact of a self-replacement policy is anybody's guess."

There was a pause. "I don't much like Danforth's idea," said Busby, "though I'll have to think about it. There's too much risk, too much uncertainty."

"Some of the senators who're toying with the idea of strategic voting feel that uncertainty may work in our favor. Passage of the self-replacement bill is one thing; implementation is another. The given senators think the bill will prove unpopular for fiscal reasons. The payments to mothers of female children will have to come from the redistribution fund for the wage subsidy program, where they will increase the amounts paid in by net contributors and reduce the subsidies paid to low earners. Much opposition can be expected. Thus we might want the payment amounts under the self-replacement bill to be left to administrative discretion, in hopes that the ultimate compromise will leave the payments too small to achieve their intended purpose."

"Fine, fine, but there's still too much risk."

"Then let me tell you about the other idea worth considering. It comes from Senator Frobish. He and his staff think we ought to vote the self-replacement bill into law, then challenge it in the Supreme Court on the grounds that it's unconstitutional."

"What in the world would that accomplish?"

"The idea is that the legal challenge would address a lot of federal actions in addition to the self-replacement bill. Over the years Progressive governments have established all sorts of statutes and administrative policies that work to male disadvantage. We've attempted to challenge them legally from time to time, but the Supreme Court has been able to avoid hearing these cases because the actions at issue weren't explicitly discriminatory. For example, there was once a statute requiring all companies to work toward an equal gender mix of board members. As more and more companies reached this condition, the statute was successively amended to cover entire industries and then the economy as a whole. Finally when the country was approaching an overall tilt toward female board members, the statute was quietly rescinded. In this fashion an area of male advantage was taken away without any action specifically favoring women. The idea is that we would oblige the Supreme Court to address many grievances of this nature by packaging them with something that's undeniably gender-discriminatory, namely the self-replacement act."

"But your example is a statute that has come and gone. We can't undo what's already been done. How much is left to protest?"

"Plenty, such as the regulations mandating gender-equal participation on all football teams, mountaineering expeditions, code-writing projects and so forth. Admittedly, the roles played by most of these traditionally male pursuits are symbolic, but that doesn't make them unimportant. Males need some things to call their own, in compensation for the life-experiences and related resources to which only females have access."

"What makes you think the Court will consider the whole package, rather than simply throwing out everything besides self-replacement?"

"The Court is weighted toward idealists who find it terribly important to view themselves as fair. Of course, discriminating against males could be considered fair from an historical perspective, since the reverse held true in all past millennia. But fortunately the given justices don't think that way. They won't be able to overlook the blatant gender discrimination involved in rewarding women for selective breeding, and once our case has their attention they'll apply their fairness criteria to the rest of it, or so we hope. The legal people consulted by Frobish suggest using an appeal analogous to that employed in the school desegregation case nearly a century and a half ago. The plaintiffs argued then that so-called 'separate but equal' schools were inherently unequal, to the disadvantage of black people, even though this characteristic wasn't written into any statutes. Our argument would be that government actions have worked to the systematic disadvantage of males regardless of their stated intent. Once they get over their pique at having to think about gender, the idealist justices on today's court might buy it."

"The odds don't seem terribly good to me."

"This may be so, but as one of my colleagues on the Hill has pointed out, we might achieve a pooling of risk. Suppose we implement both the Danforth and Frobish proposals. That is, we negotiate a version of the self-replacement bill with the population-sustaining immigration feature. This gets enacted into law with our help. Then we turn around and file suit in the manner envisioned by Frobish. This would be dirty pool, but nobody could stop us. The possible outcomes would then be as follows.

"First, the Supreme Court could throw out our entire lawsuit. This would be a worst-case situation if Danforth's people have been too optimistic in assessing the demographic impacts of the self-replacement bill. But it would require the Court to overlook the clearly unconstitutional status of that bill.

"Second, the Court could nullify the self-replacement bill in its entirely while rejecting the rest of our case. This would leave us no worse off than the option of initially failing to support the bill.

"Third, the Court could overthrow the self-replacement bill in its entirely while ruling favorably on the rest of our case. This would leave us much better off than the do-nothing alternative.

"Fourth, the Court could nullify just the reproduction-related part of the self-replacement bill while retaining its immigration feature. This would also leave us better off than doing nothing.

"And fifth, the Court could take the above action while ruling favorably on the rest of our case, which would be the best outcome of all.

"In my opinion the odds of the third, fourth and fifth outcomes collectively outweigh the odds of the first. Thus I think pursuing both the Danforth and Frobish proposals would be the best move."

"Interesting," said the Senator. "Maybe you're right."

At this point he sat up and turned to Simon. "Son, on reflection I'd better ask you not to tell anyone about what we've just discussed. If my colleagues should decide to go with such a strategy, the lawsuit will have to remain a secret until the self-replacement bill has been modified and passed."

"Sure, Dad, absolutely."

The group unwound with a few minutes of casual conversation. Then Ralph Aiken took his leave and Senator Busby and his son retired upstairs.

The next day Busby managed to meet with both senators Frobish and Danforth, although not at the same time. Frobish was aware of Danforth's proposal to introduce a population-sustaining feature into the self-replacement bill and was already in favor of combining this move with a legal challenge after the bill was passed. Danforth hadn't heard about the lawsuit idea, so Busby got someone from Frobish's staff to sit in on their meeting and explain the nature of the proposed legal action. Danforth was interested in this twist on his proposal, but wasn't quite ready to commit.

These parties agreed that a full session of the senate's Conservative caucus should meet on the matter as soon as possible. All of the Conservative senators would have to be brought up to speed beforehand on the Danforth and Frobish proposals, but for reasons of security nothing about the lawsuit idea should be put in writing. This created a need for Frobish's staff to conduct briefing sessions with the senators individually and in small groups.

Three weeks thus passed before the Conservative caucus was able to meet, with eighteen of the twenty Conservative senators present. It was a closed session in which only a few staff members were admitted and all parties were sworn to secrecy. The discussion was spirited but less acrimonious and drawn-out than many of the participants expected. The lawsuit proposal didn't require a consensus at the meeting because this legal challenge would come from outside the Senate and clearly had enough support to assure its occurrence if the self-replacement bill were passed. There was rapid agreement on the proposal to demand a population-sustaining feature in the self-replacement bill, since few of the Conservative senators could vote for the bill without this sweetener.

Hence most of the debate revolved around a motion from one of the senators that if the parties present were in favor of the amended self-replacement bill, their support should be unanimous. The argument was that they would need sixty votes to invoke cloture if the opposing Progressives mounted a filibuster against the bill. Progressive support was expected to total forty-two or forty-three votes. Some of the participants considered it unlikely that Progressives would filibuster their party's own bill, but at length the motion for unanimity won out. On this basis all eighteen of the Conservative senators in attendance pledged to vote for the amended self-replacement bill when it reached the Senate floor.

In the meanwhile the subcommittee charged with formulating the self-replacement bill had been engaged in various hearings and deliberations. It happened that the only Conservative member of this subcommittee was Senator Frank Busby. At an opportune moment, Busby took the floor and announced that the Conservative caucus was demanding a modification of the self-replacement bill as the price of its support. A new provision of the bill would have to establish a legal requirement for all successive federal administrations to manage immigration policy so that the national population remained as close as possible to the total prevailing on the date the bill was signed. Any variation from this total by more than one or two percent would render the entire self-replacement act null and void. Busby added a few comments about the possible structuring and implementation of this requirement, then sat down.

The subcommittee was thrown into an uproar, with a flurry of objections and protests coming from Progressive supporters of the bill. At length the subcommittee chair called a halt to the proceeding and declared that further deliberations would be suspended until the sponsors of the bill could respond to the Conservative demand.

Over the next several days various Progressive senators huddled to consider the situation. They could see the Conservative advantage in promoting immigration, but many of them felt there had to be some other factor behind the Conservatives' sudden willingness to support the self-replacement bill. A number of staffers were deputized to find out, using any available means, what had transpired at the top-secret caucus where the Conservative demand had originated. In a few days the most physically attractive of these spies got an answer by hooking up with one of the caucus attendees, who let slip that there was a plan to file suit against the self-replacement measure once it was enacted. This source didn't reveal any details of the proposed lawsuit, but the interested Progressives could imagine ways in which it would leave the Conservative Party better off than without the bill. They had to acknowledge that the bill was indeed unconstitutional due to its gender-discriminatory aspect; that the Supreme Court would probably be obliged to hear a case addressing this issue; and that the Court might then throw out the self-replacement act in whole or in part.

There was need for another bill. Without an alternative in place, the spontaneous propensity of mothers to substitute female for male children wouldn't be sufficient to offset the expected further declines in overall fertility, making it impossible to stabilize the population at any level without allowing immigration flows large enough to threaten the Progressives' cultural hegemony. Thus the Progressive Party had to develop a different bill that promised to tilt the future population sharply toward females while making no explicit reference to gender. Such an act would not only pass constitutional muster but garner support from both the idealist and pragmatist wings of the party, making Conservative support unnecessary.

A caucus of Progressive senators decided that development of the new bill should occur outside the subcommittee structure and appointed a working group for this purpose. The four leading members of the working group were senators Swartz, Hickey, Wenn and Boyle. Senator Hickey was male (or BP, born-with-penis, in Progressive jargon) and the other three were female (or BV, born-with-vagina). Despite being BV, Senator Boyle wasn't an especially militant feminist and thus was included to represent the more forgiving members of the party.

At the working group's first meeting, Senator Swartz took the floor and outlined the situation.

"We want to establish some law that will reward births of BV individuals, and maybe penalize BP offspring, without making any reference to g★★der in the language of the act. What human behavior or characteristic will provide the most usable distinction between BVs and BPs?"

"Well," said Senator Wenn, "there are all sorts of activities in which BV and BP individuals participate at different rates, from sewing to watching athletic contests. But measurement would pose serious problems, besides which the prospect of rewards or penalties could affect behavior. What we want is something enduring, like a physical characteristic."

"A physical characteristic such as height or body-weight could be seen as an obvious marker for g★★der and thus leave us vulnerable to legal challenge," said Swartz. "The existence of overlap between BVs and BPs wouldn't eliminate this problem and would yield some perverse outcomes. We wouldn't want to penalize a mother for bearing an especially tall BV child or reward zir for a very short BP one. We need to focus on a long-term BP identifier that's an optional—and preferably culpable—form of behavior."

"The answer is obvious," interjected Senator Hickey with a self-satisfied look. "BPs tend to avoid raising children. Most of them don't mind siring children, but they're likely to slip away afterward. The reason is their unwillingness to meet society's expectation of dual parenting, wherein the BV and BP participants play identical, indistinguishable roles from the moment of birth onwards. BP individuals are fully capable of doing this—as my own modest example demonstrates—but very often they don't."

"You're right," said Swartz. "Avoidance of child-rearing is a good BP-versus-BV discriminator and is appropriate for other reasons. But focusing on this will require our incentive system to look across generations. Our inability to reward a mother for BV children directly means that the incentive has to involve grandchildren. By establishing a reward for grandchildren and maybe a penalty for lack of them, we motivate a mother to bear BV offspring in order to maximize the likelihood of coming out ahead."

"What about grandchildren that BP children sire and then abandon?" asked Wenn.

"Obviously they shouldn't count. An individual should only receive credit for grandchildren that zir biological offspring are raising as on-site custodial parents."

"Keeping track of that for every household in the country would get mighty complicated."

"Okay, let's say there's a once-and-final determination when a child reaches a certain age, like ten or twelve. If a parent is cohabitating with a child who reaches the given age, each parent of that parent becomes eligible for reward as a grandparent. Of course, to keep the system nondiscriminatory, rewards must be granted similarly regardless of the BV-versus-BP status of parents and grandparents."

"A one-time determination of relevant parenthood will provide a convenient way to rule out grandchildren obtained via undeserving parents," said Senator Hickey. "Suppose persons W and X have a child Y, but X is not cohabiting with Y when Y reaches age ten or twelve. Our system then declares that any future children of Y cannot count as grandchildren of X. Furthermore any of those future children who reach the critical age with Y not present won't count as grandchildren of either X or W. Since parental absence is overwhelmingly a BP phenomenon, what we've done is create an extra motivation for W to bear a BV child."

"Let's summarize where we stand," said Swartz. "At the time a child is born, its two biological parents are determined by genetic testing. Keep in mind that present technology allows the biological parents to be both BV or both BP rather than a mixed couple. Then time passes. If one of the biological parents is absent when the child reaches age ten or twelve, this person is declared to have a permanent lack of grandchildren via that child. Next the child grows up and may have children of zir own. If ze is present when they reach ten or twelve, they count as grandchildren of the original biological parents, possibly excluding one who's been disqualified for reasons of absence."

"I can see problems with this," said Wenn. "Suppose—using Senator Hickey's notation—that person W has a child Y at age forty, and then person Y starts having children at age forty. (I'm assuming both W and Y are BV.) Person W doesn't start getting grandchild credits for Y's children until the first one reaches at least age ten, by which time W will be ninety years old. If W's reward for grandchildren is to be an ongoing stream of payments, ze isn't likely to receive them for very long, and if it's to be a single lifetime payment, ze may miss out altogether.

"And then there's a problem of disproportionate rewards. Let's consider the best case from society's point of view. It is what can be called the new nuclear family: two BV partners with two children, a fully self-replacing and sustainable unit. If the next generation is similar, each of the original partners will have four grandchildren. As a best case, this outcome should elicit a top reward. But the country still has an element of patriarchy, mainly associated with fundamentalist religion and recent immigration. By forcing their objects of oppression to bear many children, the patriarchal families in question can include persons with a dozen or more grandchildren. We certainly don't want to bless their atavistic lifestyle with lavish rewards.

"Even if we cap the number of rewarded grandchildren at four, there will still be an undesirable amount of variation, given that some people are bound to lose out from the system through no fault of their own. I'd like to see something binary, wherein a person is either rewarded or not. Incidentally, I think we should be talking about an ongoing stream of positive rewards, with no penalties, the way things were set up under the old self-replacement bill."

"I agree that there should only be a stream of positive rewards," said Swartz. "I also agree that a binary approach would have advantages. Let's say that each child has what we call a primary parent. Then we specify that a reward-yielding grandchild has to come through a succession of primary parents. This would reduce the number of grandchildren enough to make a binary system appropriate. A person either has grandchildren, never mind their number, or has none."

"I assume that a child has just one primary parent," said Wenn. "How would this person be determined? By flipping a coin?"

"No, a random determination would be terrible…"

"I've got it!" exclaimed Hickey. "We let the child zirself choose the primary parent. This would happen at the age when parental presence is determined. Let's make that age ten, before children tend to get rebellious. The idea is that primary-parent status—and the possibility of getting rewarded via grandchildren— would be a benefit attainable through good nurturing. Of course, a person who's absent from a child's household at the critical age could never be zir primary parent."

At this point Senator Boyle spoke up. "Requiring a child to make a choice that would confer a potential benefit on one parent but not the other could yield all sorts of bad feelings. In a typical family a ten-year-old child would generally choose its mother as primary parent. BP individuals would feel that the deck was stacked against them, so would have an even greater tendency to avoid involvement in child-rearing. Our objective here is to sustain the population, not tear families apart."

"Yes, given traditionally negligent fathering, a ten-year-old BV child would undoubtedly choose its mother as primary parent, and a BP child probably would. But this outcome isn't inevitable. There's nothing unique about mothering. My BV child relates to me in exactly the same way as to zir mother, and surely would be indifferent between me and zir mother when choosing a primary parent.

"And we can design a form of recourse into the system. Suppose a family with two parenting adults has a second child. We can specify that the primary parent of the second child is automatically the adult not chosen as primary parent by the first child. The same could hold for every successive pair of children, in the unlikely event that more should arrive. The system as thus described would not only motivate BP parents to be better fathers but give many of them an incentive to have more children.

"Furthermore the primary-parent feature would let us get around the old-age problem that Senator Wenn mentioned earlier. We've been assuming that to avoid legal challenge, the system can't reward a desirable reproductive pattern until the second generation. But the primary-parent feature should promote BV births enough to let us reward parenthood per se, in addition to rewarding eligible grandchildren. If we do this and the standard reward amount is D dollars, a person will start receiving D dollars per year when zir child reaches age ten and names zirm as primary parent, and later will start receiving two times D dollars if this child in turn becomes a primary parent. These are the only payment amounts that come into play."

"Let me get this straight," said Swartz. "I'll run through some cases using Senator Hickey's notation. Individuals W and X are domestic partners who decide to have a child. W is a BV person who will physically bear the child and thus can control its g★★der. W is motivated to choose a BV child rather than a BP because, first, a BV child will be more likely than a BP to designate W as zir primary parent, and second, a BV will be more likely than a BP to have a child in the next generation who names zirm a primary parent. So W bears a BV child whom we call Y. If W becomes Y's primary parent as expected, W starts drawing a reward of D dollars per year. If Y goes on to become the primary parent of zir own child, W starts drawing two times D dollars per year. But W keeps drawing only D dollars if Y fails to become a primary parent or doesn't have children at all. Meanwhile X is out of the running for any reward unless ze and W have another child, which would put zirm in the same position as W, or unless X forms a new parenting partnership with somebody besides W. Lastly, if for some reason Y doesn't choose W as zir primary parent, W is in the same position as X in the original case. Thus we have a system that tilts childbirth toward BV offspring, by some amount that will depend on the size of D, without making any reference to g★★der at all."

"I think we've got it," said Senator Hickey.

"I still don't like exploiting male shortcomings to achieve our demographic objective," said Senator Boyle, "rather than working proactively to help males overcome these shortcomings. But I suppose your system will do the job, along with passing constitutional muster if it's tested."

The working group wrapped up at that point. Three days later its recommendations were presented to a session of the Progressive caucus, which approved them without modification and passed them along to the relevant Senate subcommittee. There they were packaged into a proposed piece of legislation that became known as the reproductive reward bill. The major task in structuring the bill was creating an implementation regime that would track all children and record their primary-parent designations when they reached age ten. A controversial feature of the bill was a provision that these designations and the resulting payments to primary parents would begin as soon as the bill became law, rather than waiting for ten-plus years until the influence of the bill on parental choices could affect the rewards. The stated purpose was simply to advertise the existence of the system and minimize delay in reproductive responses to it.

In two more months the Senate passed the reproductive reward bill by a party-line vote of eighty to twenty. The House then supported it by a similar margin, and the President signed it into law.

Three years passed. There were some complaints about the cost of the new legislation, which everyone paid because the reward system was financed by a draw on the redistribution fund associated with the wage subsidy program. Relatively high earners had to give a bit more in that program while subsidy recipients got a bit less. Other complaints about the reproductive reward act came from groups of men who realized that payments under the act would go very largely to women. These protests were effectively shouted down by Progressive voices pointing out that no payment discrepancy would exist if males would share equitably in parental responsibilities.

One evening Senator Frank Busby came home to find his son Simon visiting from graduate school. They settled in the living room with drinks and chatted about various things until Busby brought up the big news of the day.

"Did you hear about the Supreme Court decision?" asked Busby.

"I don't keep track of anything involving the Court. With me it's all engineering, all the time."

"The case didn't draw much attention on its way to the Court and was decided practically overnight. It involved a challenge to the reproductive reward act. This was the act passed three years ago as a substitute for the self-replacement bill that Ralph Aiken and I once discussed here in your presence."

"I vaguely remember that discussion, and of course am familiar with the reproductive reward act due to the public information campaign that went along with it."

"There were several odd things about the case. The legal challenge came from a group nobody had heard of before, calling itself the Male Liberation Front. When the leaders of this group were discreetly investigated, it was discovered that at least some of them had ties to the Progressive Party. The lawsuit itself simply charged that the reproductive reward act was discriminatory in impact and intent. Unlike the action we were planning to bring against the self-replacement bill, this suit didn't link the legislation in question to a broader pattern of discrimination against men, even though many other federal laws and regulations could have been addressed on similar grounds.

"The greatest oddity was the fact that the Supreme Court heard the case it all. Nothing about the language of the reproductive reward act—which had been carefully sanitized in its preparation—required the Court to do this. Frankly, the whole thing looked like a set-up, a contrived occasion for the Supreme Court justices to drive a final spike in the heart of gender. And that's exactly what they did.

"In a unanimous finding, the Court stated that gender did not exist in any meaningful sense. It had no legal standing or operative significance. Childbirth was an isolated physiological event with no further ramifications. The ability of females to exert reproductive control was precisely offset by the burdens of pregnancy, so these circumstances were mutually cancelling in any larger calculus. Males and females had the same capabilities and resources, obliging them as groups to participate identically in all areas of life. Government laws and regulations that had differential impacts on males and females were not actionable if the differences arose from either side's failure to share full responsibility for life's duties. Et cetera, et cetera.

"You know, Simon, everything about gender—all the crazy sex-based distinctions that societies created and enforced throughout history—had one overriding objective, namely reproductive success. Feminists like to say that gender-based rules only supported reproductive success by forcing women to have babies, but that was only part of the story, and not the most important part. I won't bore you with an explanation except to say that the key linkage involved male behavior rather than female behavior. Anyway, what we've done now is redefine reproductive success to mean a level of fertility rendered sustainable by reducing the presence of men. Maybe this will work. I'm not sure I care anymore."

8

PARTY

Stokely and Alex were the last guests to arrive at the party because Alex hadn't wanted to go and had delayed their departure as long as possible. The event was celebrating the eighth birthday of a schoolmate whom Alex didn't know well and didn't especially like. Stokely would have been more than happy to pass up the occasion, but Evan had given them strict orders to attend.

Their preparations had been simplified by the lack of any need to procure and bring along a birthday present. The mother of the birthday child had notified the other parents that gift-giving would be unwelcome because this practice was materialistic and inevitably acquired a competitive aspect. On the other hand, the attending children would of course have to bring their own edible treats because no communal fare could possibly meet their varying nutritional requirements.

The birthday ice cream and cake that Stokely could remember from his own childhood had been gone for decades, banished by myriad allergies and gastric sensibilities and ideologically driven dietary regimes. The practice of lighting and blowing out candles had disappeared once there was no central foodstuff to bear them. The happy-birthday song had accordingly faded away, and the custom of having everyone eat at the same time had become unenforceable once the food ceased to be anything special. For Alex, Stokely had brought a container of some sort of custard that Evan had prepared the previous day.

Stokely and Alex were greeted by the mother of the birthday child and ushered into the party room without benefit of introductions. On entering, Stokely couldn't help noticing that he was the only father present. He had long since managed to abolish and abhor all thoughts of gender when it came to children, but he found members of his own generation harder to liberate. To him fathers were still fathers and mothers were still mothers, and the latter accounted for all the parents in attendance that afternoon besides himself. Two of the moms appeared to be trans, but he was the only current if not progenitive father.

The children numbered at least a dozen and were all seven or eight years old. Their dress could hardly have been more variable. One child wore an elaborate Middle Eastern outfit topped by a turban with an enormous fake ruby, while in contrast one wore a shapeless garment resembling a gunny sack. Most were clad in pants or tights or knickers, and their embellishments included a cape, a serape, an imitation fur boa, and various hats. Two of the children wore outfits exactly matching those of their mothers, or vice versa.

While admiring the clothing choices, Stokely noticed that a couple of the children were wearing diapers. This reflected the experts' recent emphasis on minimizing the psychic cost of toilet training. A child's gain of autonomy from learning bowel control could be more than offset by the loss of autonomy from being forced to do this, so the onset of toilet training should be the child's decision. Most made this decision before reaching school age, but some postponed it a long time because they liked the attention involved in being changed. Similar considerations prevailed with regard to breast-feeding, and Stokely knew it was possible that not all of the children present had stopped nursing.

Currently three children near the center of the party room were engaged in a loud argument, which their mothers were trying to moderate, and two were having a giggly conversation in one corner. All the other children were scattered around the room looking down at their phones. In most cases their mothers were standing by and imploring them to socialize, but they ignored these entreaties just as the mothers had ignored the earlier entreaty from the hostess to keep phones away from the party. Stokely asked Alex whose birthday was being celebrated and was pointed to one of the participants in the loud argument, who was wearing a purple sash and a rhinestone-studded tiara.

At this point the hostess, wearing a rather frantic look, clapped her hands three times to get everyone's attention. She clearly wanted to start some kind of group activity, but hadn't settled upon anything in particular. Several mothers gathered around and started offering suggestions, all of which met with immediate objections from other mothers. The children could play a game, but contests like dodge-ball and musical chairs were too violent, and anything athletic would devolve into a celebration of ableism. Games were bad in any case because they produced winners and losers. Activities that required children to speak up or otherwise perform individually would place the slower and shyer ones at risk of embarrassment and loss of self-esteem.

During this conference the tiara-wearing birthday child left the room and came back carrying a guitar. After getting the attention of zir mother, who shushed the other mothers, ze made the following announcement.

"It's my party, so everybody can listen to me play my guitar."

With great concentration ze pressed the guitar strings with zir left hand and stroked them with zir right, first tentatively and then twice more with increasing emphasis. Then ze carefully rearranged the left-hand fingers and strummed a different chord several times. Between intermittent pauses there followed more chords, pleasing enough in themselves but not conveying any sort of tune.

The room was initially quiet, but in a minute or two the other children became restive and broke out in several conversations. Indeed they seemed more inclined to talk now that they had something to interrupt. As the sound of young voices increased, the birthday child responded by striking the guitar strings louder and louder, soon forgetting to produce intelligible chords. The rising cacophony was then pierced by a voice yelling, "That's terrible!" This touched off an ebullient chorus of boos and jeers that lasted until the birthday child threw down zir guitar and fled from the room in tears.

The hostess followed her child out of the room, but soon returned in unhappy acknowledgment of her need to carry on with the party. She made a shrill reference to music and got something playing on her audio system. It was a children's song, and she started singing along with it in hopes that the youngsters would join in. Several did, but their efforts trailed off when they looked around and saw that most of the children had gone back to their phones. Singing progressively louder, the hostess started waving her arms like an orchestra conductor, which only managed to launch some other mothers into brief snatches of song.

As the singing faded away, one of the mothers who hadn't been participating suggested brightly, "Maybe they'd like to dance! Put on something lively!"

The hostess abruptly changed the music to a rock 'n roll number with a pounding beat. She turned up the volume until few if any children could still pay attention to their phones, then started dancing erratically across the room. None of the children joined in until several mothers took theirs by the hand and managed to get them moving. Gradually some more children and mothers came forth, while others stepped back to make way for them.

Then a voice rose above the music, yelling: "No! I don't *want* to dance! I want to watch *you!*" It came from a child whose mother was holding zir hand and urging zirm to participate. In alarm the given mother let go and started to dance on her own. Her efforts were so timid and spasmodic that they caught the attention of two nearby children who stopped dancing to watch as well. This spurred a general realization that watching mothers dance was more fun than doing it one's self. Soon all of the children had stopped moving, and nearly all were ordering their mothers to dance, and nearly all of the mothers were complying.

The talents of the dancing mothers varied a great deal. A few were rhythmic and graceful; some managed to keep time in a perfunctory way; and some were ludicrous. Attention was inexorably drawn to the last group. In a moment the children were bunched around the most dancing-challenged moms, whose efforts they mocked with much finger-pointing and snide commentary and ribald imitation. A few of the other mothers stopped dancing when they were no longer being watched, but most kept on moving as ordered.

The star of the event turned out to be a mother who was very fat. Her dancing consisted of random bumps and grinds that had nothing to do with the music. Each time her body went up and down, her rolls of fat jiggled and swayed and fought each other for domination. The children around her—who came to include the entire group—started shouting "BUMP! BUMP! BUMP!" along with the beat that the fat mom was ignoring. She started sweating heavily and then began to stagger.

Abruptly the hostess stopped the music. For a moment the room was completely quiet.

Then came a voice saying, "I'm going home!" The speaker headed for the door followed by zir mother. Almost immediately the other children started departing. There was no need to say goodbye to the birthday child, if anyone was so inclined, because ze had never returned to the party room after the guitar episode.

Stokely, who'd been hiding in a corner to avoid the dancing, was entrained by Alex and left in the middle of the pack. Once they were outside, Alex would only say that the party had gone pretty much as expected.

9

TRANS

Stokely had always been happy enough with Evan as a sexual partner. He was well suited for monogamy, being a person who liked routine and was easily unsettled by surprises. But as a believer in all things progressive, Evan felt that everyone had a moral obligation to be bisexual. Thus she kept a girlfriend on the side and insisted that Stokely have periodic relations with another man. In complying with this demand, Stokely was constrained by the fact that he didn't particularly like being sodomized. Eventually he worked out a satisfactory relationship with a self-described homosexual named Buster, a passive individual who was happy to have Stokely provide all the ministrations on both sides.

One evening after Alex had been put to bed, Evan drifted into conversation about her female partner, a somewhat younger woman named Sport.

"There's been a change in our relationship. Ze…"

"Please spare me the politically correct referents. The whole point of Sport is that she's a woman, so let her be avowedly female."

"Okay. She has recently taken a male lover."

"So what's the problem? You've got one of those too. Anyway, I thought Sport didn't like men."

"Sport doesn't like men—the overall male package—but she does like penises. The problem is that her new partner is a special sort of man with a lot to offer in that area. He's got one of those new bionic penises. An implant, which Sport described in great detail. Its characteristics such as length, diameter, contours, temperature, surface texture and optional vibration are all adjustable. The unit is wired into its bearer's central nervous system and thus has three different operational modes. When the bearer places it in piloted mode, he mind-controls all of the abovementioned variables based on any criteria he may choose. When he places it in automatic mode, the unit's onboard computer optimizes its performance characteristics—other than rhythm, which remains the bearer's responsibility—in real-time response to vaginal conditions as reported by its myriad sensors.

"Sport's favorite is manual mode. This third option is enabled by the installation of a port in the bearer's lower back. For manual mode a control panel is plugged into this port and placed wherever the recipient of penile attention may choose. Sport likes having intercourse in missionary position with the control panel nestled under her fingertips between the bearer's buns. This gives her something she's always wanted: a designer penis under her absolute, moment-to-moment command. She's described to me in exhaustive and exhausting detail the ecstasies thus obtainable."

"You're afraid she won't want you anymore?"

"No, she'll always want me, because I can give her the one thing that's beyond male capability and can't be automated."

"What's that?"

"Cunnilingus. Sport insists that only a woman has the knowledge to do this properly. She says I'm one of the best."

"So again, what's the problem? She's got her bionic plaything, and you've got me, and the rest of the time you've got each other."

"The problem is that her new exposure has made her unsatisfied with my limitations. She's very fond of me and would like to have me fulfill all her sexual needs. She wants me to do that by getting my own bionic penis for intermittent use. The type of unit she has in mind is a plug-in, not an implant, and is designed for a female bearer. It's got some sort of protuberance for vaginal insertion plus an external harness to provide stability. Since it's not connected to the bearer's nervous system, it can only run in automatic or manual mode rather than piloted mode. Sport would just want access to its control panel.

"She says that if I truly cared about her I would procure such a unit for her satisfaction. Cost is not an issue since the National Health Service covers both plug-in and implanted bionic penises under its Pursuit of Sexual Happiness imperative. According to Sport, obtaining a bionic member would make me the ideal sexual partner: a woman in a man's body, or something like that. But I'm just not interested in wielding a penis. I'm not constitutionally set up to give pleasure that way and would surely do a bad job of it regardless of Sport's control-panel virtuosity. She refuses to accept my decision on this matter, and her insistence is beginning to sour our whole relationship."

"Surely this issue will blow over in a while. As it happens, I've got a somewhat similar problem with Buster.

"Buster is very unstable, as I've described to you more than once. He goes off on flights of fancy that he takes with utmost seriousness until something else comes along. Up until now he's been firmly committed to gay sex. In fact, to increase its rewards he recently had the National Health Service give him one of those three-way sphincters with orgasmic capability. This implant seemed to make him very happy. But now all of a sudden he's saying he wants a sex change.

"The driver isn't a desire to be a woman so much as a conviction that he is deeply, desperately in love with me. He's sure I would like him better as a female. He may even dream of taking me away from you to become his full-time partner. I've tried endlessly to explain that I don't want or need another woman and might not even be attracted to him, or rather her, in that form. But to no avail. He has already started taking hormones to launch the transgender process."

"It sounds like you'll have to stop seeing him altogether."

"I want a sex change!" This voice came from the staircase that descended to the living room from the house's upper floor. Stokely and Evan turned to see eight-year-old Alex sitting on one of the upper stairs, where ze had apparently been listening to their conversation.

Stokely sat open-mouthed while Evan considered her response. At length she said, "I don't see how you can talk about gender reassignment when at your age you effectively don't have a gender. We have done everything possible to isolate you from sexist contamination. We raised you according to the Swedish Method wherein you were never told whether you were a girl or boy. All of your schools and play groups were carefully chosen to be gender-free. Do you even know which of your classmates are girls and which are boys?"

"I know about half of them. A few have told me, and some I can tell by looking."

"Say," interrupted Stokely, "how about describing your present gender situation."

"I'm a boy. I want to be a girl."

"Why?"

"I want to grow up like Mom. She seems happier than you."

Along with being stung by this observation, Stokely had a flash of sexist regret that he hadn't done anything to make the manly estate more appealing. He suppressed these feelings and said, "All you have to do to become a girl at this stage is tell everybody you're a girl. You're in an environment where this won't make any difference to how you act or how you look, but go ahead and do it if it makes you feel better. There's no reason why you can't pass for a female."

"Gender reassignment surgery is out of the question at your age," said Evan. "You can't be equipped with adult sex organs until you're an adult, or something close. Such organs provide the only meaningful definition of gender—and even that is debatable—so you might as well think of yourself as genderless until you get them. Make a choice if you like, but don't take it seriously."

After a bit more discussion they sent Alex back to bed and then retired themselves. Several days later Evan got the idea that she should try to talk Buster out of having a sex change for Stokely's sake. At least a joint meeting with the married couple might convince Buster that Even was and would remain Stokely's only woman. They invited Buster to the house, then were joined unexpectedly by Sport, who dropped by to show Evan some literature extolling the glories of the bionic penis. The four of them got into a wide-ranging conversation and then wound up in bed together.

The romantic foursome was unexciting for Evan and Stokely but eye-opening for the other two participants.

Buster told the group that he wasn't really gay; he avoided sex with women because one of them had once insulted his penis. He generally didn't like women—the overall female package—but he did like vaginas. This news led to a session of cunnilingus with Sport that the latter found miraculous. She couldn't believe any male could be so *sensitive*. Meanwhile Buster announced that his anti-female posture didn't apply to Sport because he found her so deliciously commanding.

Sport and Buster weren't seen for two months after that. Then they showed up hand-in-hand on Evan's and Stokely's doorstep. Buster was a man reborn, having gotten himself implanted with a shiny new bionic penis. It was the latest model with additional capabilities such as an ability to rotate and go around corners. Sport and Buster were now made for each other. Marriage and children beckoned, and Evan and Stokely wished them well.

Evan found herself another girlfriend in a short period of time. Stokely hasn't reestablished his bisexuality yet, but will surely get around to it.

10

CORRECT

"In 1991 the University of Michigan held a conference to address the alleged emergence of a dogmatic viewpoint known as 'political correctness.' After much deliberation, the attending scholars decided there was no such thing as political correctness, but if there were, it would be correct."

Nobody laughed. These lines, which had always opened Professor Bingham's annual lecture on political correctness, had gotten less and less response over the years and now were met with complete silence. The problem may have been that few contemporary college students had ever heard of political correctness. The phrase had fallen out of use because the more extreme aspects of the phenomenon were long gone, while its underlying thrust had fully blended into mainstream thought and behavior. Bingham took note of the need to start the lecture differently next time, if there was a next time.

"In the popular conception of political correctness, the term 'correctness' connoted rigid adherence to a detailed orthodoxy, and the 'political' elements of that orthodoxy were left-wing. This definition was accurate as far as it went, but greatly understated the scope of the phenomenon. Political correctness was political in a very broad sense, extending far beyond the issues addressed in electoral contests. The driving force was not the nation's ongoing left-right schism but its emerging gender realignment. Political correctness arose as a declaration of war on patriarchy..."

"Excuse me!" The upraised hand belonged to Darnell, the only student in the class who seemed to pay attention and keep up with the readings. "Your book's chapter on political correctness treated it as something different from alliance with the progressive wing of the Democratic Party, but I can't help thinking that 'politically correct' was just a pejorative descriptor of progressive views."

"Well, you're right that there was a convergence of political correctness and the positions of the Democratic Party's left wing. But the point in my book was that the attitudes of progressive Democrats converged to fit the gender-driven dictates of political correctness rather than vice versa. An example involved postures toward international conflict. For over half of the twentieth century, Democrats were more willing than Republicans to get involved in foreign wars. Then when the flowering of gender consciousness identified warfare as an element of male-pattern aggression, the Democrats became the more dovish party and maintained this position thereafter. Before getting into details, however, let me finish describing the origins of political correctness."

The book Darnell mentioned was Bingham's main scholarly contribution. It covered America's cultural transition from the nineteen-fifties through the twenty-teens and had gotten some favorable notice for its treatment of gender conflict as a fundamental driver. But the book was now thirty years old and had no audience other than the students whom Bingham forced to read it. Bingham's work had long been out of favor because it lacked the triumphalism that permeated later studies of the emergent progressive hegemony. Bingham himself was considered suspect, and his courses were less and less popular, but the university was letting him stay around on the premise that he would soon retire.

"The epochal event was the coming of birth control. Demographically, birth control meant that the concern of advanced countries would inevitably shift from having too many children to having too few. Culturally, birth control would liberate women from traditional roles and increase their impact in every area of society. The year 1960 can be viewed as a milestone in this regard because it brought the arrival of safe, effective and female-administrable contraception in the form of the birth control pill."

"But," interrupted Darnell, "birth control had been around for a long time before 1960."

"Indeed, various methods had been used since antiquity, but not until well into the twentieth century did any of them come close to meeting all the criteria just mentioned. There were also a lot of social and institutional barriers to the use of birth control, which wasn't even legal in all the U.S. states until 1962. The arrival of the pill created enough pressure to sweep away these constraints and open the doors to sexual and reproductive freedom.

"Over the course of the 1960s the most visible impacts of birth control were a flurry of divorce, a rise in sexual adventurism, and a plunge in the birth rate. Then the 1970s brought the entry of huge numbers of U.S. women into the labor force. Feminism gathered strength during these years, but the limits of the organized women's movement were shown by the failure of the Equal Rights Amendment in 1977-82.

"Political correctness arrived in the late 1980s. My own research placed its birth in precisely 1988, although this date was never widely accepted. The onset of a gender-based cultural insurgency was marked by a concatenation of events having little to do with traditional concerns of the women's movement and nothing to do with electoral politics. There was a sudden upsurge in campaigns against hazards like drunk driving that had existed at constant or declining intensities for decades. Women subjected themselves to hypnosis and other suggestive therapies in order to report lurid 'recovered memories' of childhood abuse. Date rape supplanted street crime as a perceived sexual threat. Some colleges started requiring male students to obtain written agreements before making any amorous advances. These events all cropped up around 1988, and what they had in common was fear of the masculine presence. The male archetype had shifted from daddy the protector to daddy the abuser. The enemy was patriarchy, and the battle was joined.

"These early developments and their subsequent flowering into full-blown political correctness occurred largely in the media and on college campuses. If they had remained within these confines, we wouldn't be talking about them now, but inevitably they didn't.

"Political correctness involved a consistent array of attitudes toward practically everything. For the rest of this hour I'll be talking about what created this consistency, namely what formed the basis for preferring one side of each dichotomy over the other. The dichotomies in question had to do with ideals, beliefs, intellectual postures, and patterns of thought, plus their reflections in choice and behavior. For simplicity I refer to all these entities as 'values'."

Darnell's hand went up. "Weren't people's 'values' limited to things they especially cared about? You make it sound as if the average person cared about everything."

"I'm using 'values' as an omnibus term to cover all the things that people could favor or disfavor other than material objects. Your observation is well taken, because one of the messages of political correctness was indeed that people should care about everything, or at least everything within their purview. They were encouraged to form preferences wherever possible and maintain these likes and dislikes in strict alignment with other correct sentiments. This will become clearer momentarily.

"Values had always tended to be gender-loaded. Typically there existed a polarity between opposing or contrasting values, wherein one end of the polarity was male-associated and the other was female-associated. These polarities came from myriad sources. Some merely reflected objective differences between males and females, such as those involving size and strength and propensity for violence. Some reflected male behaviors imparted or encouraged by the patriarchal system, such as dominance and the use of force, while others reflected characteristics of that system, such as social hierarchy and its concomitants. Some of the polarities expressed male and female tendencies acquired from millennia of role specialization and female subjugation. Some reflected the cumulative influence of gender-based conflict on political orientation, and some were just tactical constructs used for various purposes in the gender war.

"Political correctness consisted of promoting or extolling the female side of every value polarity and putting down the male side. The details could get complicated, but in essence that's all there was to it. If patriarchal authority made men judgmental while motherhood made women merciful, then mercy and forgiveness should trump rules and punishment. If Man the Hunter ate meat, one should emulate Woman the Gatherer and be vegetarian. If Western religions were patriarchal, it was best to become a Buddhist. And so forth.

"Page 147 of my book offers a partial but suggestive list of relevant gender-associated values. This list reflects conditions in the 1990s when the flowering of political correctness reached its apogee, and some of the items must be understood in terms of the politics of that time. For example, literary criticism came into play because many of the leading developers of feminist theory were professors in English departments. These parties accordingly seized upon literary deconstruction, a mode of analysis that denied an author the right to say what was going on in his own text, because they liked its anti-authoritarian thrust. Postmodernism, a broad critical approach that reacted against objective efforts to explain reality, was celebrated as a counter to male-pattern thinking.

"Some of the items may appear paradoxical in combination with others. For example, an odd consequence of the culture war was the emergence of determinism as a female value, because it invalidated assignments of blame that had traditionally served patriarchal ends. This placed males on the side of free will, even though freedom per se was not in their bailiwick.

"I should note that the list omits many of the verbal hallmarks of political correctness because they're hard to express as value polarities. These tend to involve avoidance of terms that might sound like indictments or otherwise hurt people's feelings. Examples include referring to 'undocumented' rather than 'illegal' immigrants and failing to mention religion when describing terrorists. At one time this verbal delicacy reached ridiculous lengths such as calling short people 'vertically challenged.' But less extreme forms of euphemistic language have been among the most enduring aspects of political correctness and serve today as indicators of how successfully the culture has been feminized."

"Dr. Bingham," interjected Darnell. "Something struck me when I was looking over the list last night. Political correctness consisted of putting down everything male, but I've gathered from other parts of your book that a lot of women in those days were trying to be like men. They wanted to be powerful, authoritarian and so forth. So was maleness a bad thing or a good thing?"

"The situation was indeed somewhat paradoxical. A possible explanation would be that the women denigrating maleness and the women imitating it were different groups. A less charitable guess would be that people leading the cultural insurgency had different standards for men and women, so that whatever was blameworthy in men was okay for women. Perhaps the fairest view, however, is that political correctness was targeted at extremes. The objective was to draw the two sexes together toward some sort of golden mean on all the various polarities. This would require women to become more like traditional males, but not to a culpable extent. Today's cultural leaders would argue that this outcome has been pretty much achieved, which is why political correctness is now unobtrusive if not fully gone.

Twelve Pillars of Correctness

Selected Gender Polarities

Male	Female	Male	Female
perp	victim	hardness	softness
strength	weakness	bigness	smallness
hunter	gatherer	fight or flight	tend & befriend
force	suasion	violence	nurturance
authority	freedom	hierarchy	equality
command	consensus	justice	mercy
punishment	forgiveness	discipline	permissiveness
conditional love	unconditional love	conformity	diversity
territoriality	openness	tribalism	outreach
xenophobia	multiculturalism	ownership	sharing
competitiveness	collegiality	rules & drill	self-expression
self-criticism	self-esteem	dominance and sadomasochism	intersubjectivity
logic	intuition	free will	determinism
objectivity	subjectivity	logophallocentricity	postmodernism
narrative authority	literary deconstruction	factualism	perspectivism
moral absolutism	moral relativism	religious authority	humanism
original sin	primal innocence	Western religions	Eastern religions
heterosexuality	pansexuality	gender polarity	androgyny
rigidity	spontaneity	repression	liberation
bigotry	tolerance	incarceration	rehabilitation
school tracking	inclusion	product functionality	product safety
protection from others	protection from self	personal responsibility	social responsibility
flesh-eating	vegetarianism	animal products	animal rights
capitalism	socialism	economic inequality	economic justice
management	labor	exploitation	conservation
left brain	right brain	deduction	induction
linear thinking	nonlinear thinking	incorrect	sustainable
war	peace	love	hate

147

"Though very incomplete, this listing of the gender polarities enlisted by political correctness suggests the extent to which it once spanned the social and intellectual landscape. Patriarchy was everywhere and had to be confronted everywhere. Anything tinged with maleness required an antithesis, to be crafted for oppositional purposes if not already in existence. Many of the contexts were relevant only to a small and well-educated fraction of the populace, but their diversity reflected the energy behind the larger feminizing movement.

"Some general comments are required on the subjects of religion and thought and sexuality. Rejection of organized religion was a central feature of the gender-driven insurgency, even though women may have been more spiritually inclined than men. This held because monotheistic Western religions were supportive of patriarchy—starting with their implication that a single god had to be male—and because religious doctrine was often invoked in opposition to social change. Traditional male domination of economic and intellectual life had given masculine associations to many patterns of thought. Logic, rationality, objectivity, and allegiance to observable truth were male, whereas intuition, emotionalism, subjectivity, and willed truth were female. Everything on the male side was rendered suspect by the culture war, to the extent that during the peak period even practitioners of the hard sciences would sometimes question the existence of any objective reality. The bugaboo of masculine, fact-based thinking came to be known as logophallocentricity.

"Sexuality was an area of special complication because male interests were divided and could be attacked on multiple levels. Males as individuals generally favored sexual activity, especially after birth control lowered its repercussions, but female sexuality had always been problematic for whole societies. Reproductive success meant not only producing children but getting both genders to support them, which was easiest when males could claim paternity with some assurance. Thus as societies progressed beyond simple communal arrangements, the female sex drive became hazardous, and once there was enough patriarchal control to eliminate the reproductive need for it, steps were very often taken to reduce it. In the late twentieth century, sexual prudery and repression and inhibition were dissipating fast but still around. Such traits were mostly borne by females and disapproved by individual males, yet they amounted to male values because they served patriarchal ends. Conversely, sexual liberation was perhaps sought and certainly exercised more by males than females, yet it entered the culture war as a female value.

"The origins and roles of the table's other polarities can be worked out easily enough. For example, environmental activism addressed serious real-world concerns but verged into pantheistic observance and functioned as a conduit for indictment of male rapacity. A hallmark of the culture war was that the insurgents controlled not only the mainstream public forum but the language in which issues were framed. 'Homophobia' was a shrewd innovation that said opposition to any initiative for homosexuals could only be based on fear. 'Sustainable' began life as an objective descriptor of non-resource-exhausting actions, but progressively acquired filters of political correctness so that nothing offensive to progressive sensibilities could be so designated.

"In their linguistic heyday the insurgents were able to place the revolutionary forces firmly on the side of love while the reactionaries stood for hate. And in this they were quite right. Phenomena like tribalism, territoriality, and xenophobia were always part of the patriarchal heritage because it involved support groups that inevitably came into conflict. The upside of patriarchy—indeed its only excuse—was its role as a formula for reproductive success. So the remnants of patriarchy at the end of the last century were accompanied by intergroup animosity and relatively large numbers of children. The 1990s slogan "hate is not a family value" may have helped to promote social change, but hate was indeed a family value, as shown by its subsequent decline in parallel with average family size."

"Exactly who were the practitioners of political correctness?" asked Darnell. "Was it strictly a female exercise, or did men get into the act?"

"You're asking about the connection between physical gender and what I call ideological gender. We can imagine the latter as involving a continuum with male-valued individuals at one end and female-valued individuals at the other. A person's nearness to the female end would reflect how much his or her thoughts and behaviors corresponded to the dictates of political correctness, with mere lip service to it carrying little weight in the assignment. Your question can then be addressed by considering people near the two ends of the continuum and ignoring a substantial number in the middle. Then the answer is that even at the peak of social polarization, the correspondence between ideological gender and physical gender was quite rough. Male-valued women and female-valued men were perhaps half as numerous in aggregate as persons following the expected pattern.

"Values tended to converge within households, and a majority of multi-person households at the end of the last century were still headed by two adults of different genders. These circumstances plus the lingering female weakness for monotheistic religion could explain the existence of many male-valued women. Different factors applied to female-valued men because males were the people under pressure to change. Some men saw little cost in turning away from traditional male postures in order to honor abstract principles of fairness or make women happier. Some sought to curry female favor for more selfish reasons, and some of course were female-valued to begin with.

"A telling pattern was that men with postgraduate education mostly occupied the female side of the value spectrum, and at the highest educational levels a great majority of men were ideologically female. The explanation involved the male cult, male gender heroism, and other factors outside the scope of this course. Basically, education reduced the psychic cost of conforming to political correctness because it gave males alternative sources of personal heroism.

"Political correctness as an observable phenomenon reached its apogee near the end of the last century. Thereafter its linguistic excesses were curbed, its more irrational elements were abandoned, and its mission evolved into the less-obtrusive process of social feminization that continues today.

"Regarding our next class, I've been asked in past years to provide some material illustrating how political correctness registered in popular culture, so your reading assignment for next time is a novel chosen for this purpose. I recommend scanning though most of the text to get its general drift and then paying close attention to the ending."

11

LOVE STORY

"Today I'll be talking about a book called *Cold Mountain*. Have any of you had a chance to look at it?"

One hand went up, predictably belonging to Darnell. There was a flicker of movement from the back of the room that might have come from another hand, but Professor Bingham couldn't be sure. He noted that attendance in the class was even lower than in previous weeks and seemed to be headed asymptotically toward zero.

"In retrospect this book may not have been a great choice. The 1990s produced far more egregious examples of political correctness, particularly among the motion pictures of that time. The setting for Cold Mountain was the American South during the late period of the Civil War. Given such a context—a society engaged in violent defense of slavery—the writer didn't have to work very hard to establish lots of male villainy, and the times when he went overboard didn't always stand out."

"Excuse me," interjected Darnell, "but wasn't the Civil War about more than slavery?"

"There used to be some debate about that. The alternative theories mostly held that the causes of the war were economic. The South was agrarian and the North was industrial, and federal policies were systematically favoring the latter activities over the former. But given that the South's agrarian economy was largely based on slavery, one can still call it the ultimate driver. At any rate racial politics have long established that the war was all about slavery.

"I've picked *Cold Mountain* to illustrate political correctness out of admiration for the sly way the narrative is constructed. The book seems to be telling one story, but the reader finds out in the last four pages that it's really been telling another. Incidentally, it was a very successful book: selling three million copies, winning the National Book Award, and getting made into a major motion picture. None of the reviewers seemed to appreciate the significance of the turnabout in the last four pages, but you can judge this for yourself.

"The book's action takes place in 1864 and perhaps the first few days of 1865, within a year of the war's end. The plot turns on various events before the war, which we learn through recollections of the main

characters, so I'll summarize the backstory before joining the main action. In the late 1850s a young woman
named Ada has moved with her father from Charleston
to a farm in the mountains of western North Carolina.
The father, a preacher, has made this move for health
reasons and has no interest in farming. He takes over
a small church and supports the household largely on
income from past investments, employing local labor to
run the farm. He is a kindly sort whose religious posture is temperate enough to shield him from the digs
at organized religion that occur throughout the book.

"Sometime in the winter of 1860-61, Ada meets the
young male protagonist—Inman—at a dance. There is a
brief and rather constrained romance. Inman is smitten
from the outset, but Ada has a long history of rejecting
suitors and seems much more guarded. Soon the war
starts and Inman volunteers for duty. There is a faltering
goodbye scene that elicits no tears or promises, but then
Ada goes back to see Inman again and stages a warmer
performance, which includes a single goodbye kiss.

"We rejoin the two characters in the summer of
1864. After surviving horrendous battles, Inman has
been wounded very seriously in the neck and taken to
a hospital in Raleigh. There he has managed to recover
and is worried that he will soon be sent back to the
front. So he acquires some civilian clothes, escapes from
the hospital, and heads out for home. Meanwhile Ada's
father has died, leaving her destitute. Her farm is in
terrible shape, and she has no clue how to make it
productive.

"The book then follows the lives of Inman and Ada in alternating chapters. Inman is trying to make his way west across a treacherous landscape toward a destination identified as Cold Mountain. (This North Carolina peak gains stature in the telling; it's actually not even the highest mountain on its ridge.) What makes the landscape especially treacherous is something called the Home Guard. This is a militia charged by the state with hunting down deserters and other 'outliers' from the war. As described by the book, the Home Guard units are ragtag groups of vigilantes who show little interest in making arrests—as opposed to simply shooting any able-bodied men they encounter—and who enjoy looting the homes of people they claim to be Federal sympathizers. Torturing farm wives for information about hidden valuables is all in a day's work.

"Free-floating male malevolence isn't limited to the Home Guard. Early in his journey, Inman is attacked for no identifiable reason by three men who try to kill him when he resists. He manages to escape and travels to a river with a ferry crossing. The ferry isn't operating due to high water, but Inman hires the ferry-keeper's young daughter to take him across in a canoe. After they get underway in the fitful moonlight, the three men who had assaulted Inman earlier show up and start firing on the canoe with a rifle. Soon the canoe is leaking so badly that Inman and the girl have to climb out and float down the river using it as cover. Inman can see the three attackers at the ferry landing 'jumping up and down' in rage."

"That's really stupid!" interrupted Darnell. "The three guys have absolutely nothing to gain by firing on the canoe, since they can't get to Inman's belongings even if they kill him, and they don't seem to care about the possibility of shooting a local girl in the process."

"The text does go over the top from time to time. Anyway, back in the mountains Ada is practically starving on her farm when salvation arrives in the form of Ruby, a remarkable young woman who has been living nearby. Ruby offers to form an equal partnership with Ada in operating and rehabilitating the farm. From the beginning Ada is 'enormously cheered' by Ruby and impressed with her 'willing heart' and her 'spark as bright and hard as one struck with steel and flint.' We hear that Ruby was born a motherless child to a ne'er-do-well father who would leave her alone in the wilderness for months at a time. As a result, Ruby not only can do everything on a farm but knows all about nature as well. Her mystic connection with the biosphere enlists Ada in a lot of rhapsodizing about nature that permeates the text. Even Inman contributes to this after he gets out of the fetid flatlands (poisoned by slavery, one gathers) and into his beloved mountains, giving the whole book a pantheistic aura.

"At any rate Ruby and Ada get busy on Ada's farm and soon render it productive. Ruby is a tireless worker and stern taskmaster and relentless teacher, but Ada responds positively in all respects. The two develop strong bonds of friendship and affection. Their situation improves so rapidly that by the end of summer Ada says 'she could not see how she could improve her world.'

"Meanwhile Inman is still moving across central North Carolina, encountering various types of people and having various adventures. At one point he stops a preacher named Veasey from murdering a young woman bearing his child. Then Inman falls in with a 'jumble of people wearing about every tinge of skin there is,' who include outliers and a tribe of Irish gypsy horse traders. These people are happy to feed and accommodate him, initiating a pattern in which the females and people of color whom Inman encounters are invariably kind and supportive—and usually admirable—in politically correct contrast to most white males. The white outliers like Inman are a mixed bag, but tend to be good guys by virtue of their stance against the war.

"In his further travels Inman unwillingly acquires the companionship of Veasey, the amoral preacher, whom he stops from robbing a store and saves from getting shot. Together they help a man named Junior remove a threat to the local water supply, and in return are invited to Junior's home. This turns out to be an establishment so debauched that, in a rather heavy metaphor, the whole house is tilted to such an extent that chairs slide across the floor. There are nefarious characters and strange goings-on, during which we learn that Junior has murdered several people including his own mother. Inman is drugged and subjected to lascivious advances by Junior's wife, Lila, after which Junior takes Inman prisoner and the Home Guard shows up.

It happens that Junior has an arrangement with the Guard to turn over outliers for a price. Inman and Veasey are tied onto a string of other prisoners, and the Guardsmen proceed to have a drunken party. Then Junior insists on staging a wedding between Inman and Lila because she had been coming on to him."

"That's maybe the stupidest thing in the book," said Darnell. "Why have a wedding when Lila is already married and Inman has already been handed over to the Home Guard?"

"The same chapter has a couple more contenders. Inman and Veasey are taken away with the Home Guard's other prisoners and marched somewhere for a period described as several days. Then and only then do the Guardsmen decide for no particular reason to shoot them all. Why march them around first? The shooting kills Veasey and the other prisoners, but what inflicts Inman turns out to be survivable. It's a miraculous head injury in which the bullet has left entry and exit wounds in his scalp but hasn't bothered anything underneath. After the Guardsmen have left, Inman wakes up and cuts himself loose and heads on down the road.

"The chapters focusing on Ada continue to talk about farming and nature and Ruby's myriad offerings. The emotional bonds between Ada and Ruby continue to strengthen. On page 242 we find the women braiding each other's hair, and on page 373 they share their first embrace. Life on the farm is increasingly idyllic, and Ada approaches a state of happiness. On page

289 she says that 'hard times seemed far away,' and on page 327 she writes a Charleston friend that 'my new mien…is somehow akin to contentment.' Her chapters include extensive ruminations on her past life, some of which involve Inman. For most of the book these reflections are wistful rather than anguished, although there is an escalation on page 344 when Ada responds to a letter from Inman by answering with the words 'come back.' Inman's posture is more consistent; the brief references to Ada in his chapters make clear that his quest involves reuniting with her as well as Cold Mountain.

"Inman succeeds in reaching the mountains and is taken in by a character referenced as the goatwoman. She is an old lady living alone with her goats who is regarded as so admirable that she gets nearly a whole chapter. Her backstory is that as a young woman she was forcibly married to an old man who, following a well-established pattern, was likely to kill her 'from work and babies and meanness.' So she escaped to the hills and took up residence in a cart where she's lived ever since. She is a nature-worshipping opponent of war and slavery who stands as an archetype of the enlightened independent female.

"Further down the road Inman is taken in by another woman who has a baby and a hog that needs slaughtering. After a night in her care, Inman is roused by the approach of raiders. As an equal-opportunity disparager of all things martial, the author has made these raiders Federal troops rather than agents of the

Confederacy. Inman takes cover nearby and is forced to watch as the raiders loot the house and threaten to let the baby die if the woman won't tell where her valuables are hidden. At length they give up on finding anything special, so they ride off with everything handy including the hog. Inman follows the raiders and manages to kill all three of them. He returns with the hog, which he and the woman proceed to slaughter, then spends another night with her before moving on.

"Over the next several days Inman helps another woman bury her dead baby; finds three skeletons hanging pointlessly from a hemlock tree; and moves into high mountain country that he's beginning to recognize."

"Don't forget the bear," interjected Darnell.

"Right," said Bingham. "Why don't you tell about the bear."

"Okay. It seems that while fighting in the war Inman had dreamed of being turned into a bear and finding peace in that condition. From this he concluded that bears had something hopeful to teach and vowed he would never kill one 'no matter what the expense.' Then in the mountains he finds himself backed up against a cliff getting charged by a mama bear. What to do? The book says: 'Inman took a step to the side and the bear rushed by him and plunged over the high ledge...' So we learn that if you're getting charged by a bear, all you have to do is step aside. Once the mama bear is just as dead as if Inman had shot her, he shoots and eats the accompanying baby bear, which is okay since it has no chance of survival, and moves on in smug belief that he's kept his high-minded vow."

"Back at Ada's farm," resumed Bingham, "things are complicated by the arrival of Ruby's long-lost father, whom she catches stealing corn. The father—whose name is Stobrod—has deserted from the army and is living with a bunch of other outliers in a mountain cave. After the initial encounter, Stobrod visits the farm on occasion and eventually is forgiven, at Ada's insistence, for his neglectful fathering of Ruby. He is just as worthless as ever except that he has become amazingly adept as a fiddle-player, which in the story gives him a sort of transcendence.

"Stobrod introduces two additional characters from the outlier cave. One is Pangle, a simple-minded banjo player who serves as Stobrod's accompanist. The other is Reid, a part-Indian boy of 'no more than seventeen' who was conscripted in Georgia and, having deserted from the Army, is trying ineffectively to get back. Stobrod is now avoiding Ada's farm for fear of encountering the Home Guard, but Ruby promises to leave food for him and Pangle at an appointed spot. After a visit to this spot they head deeper into the mountains with Reid tagging along.

"Several days later Stobrod and Pangle are surprised in camp by a band of Home Guard scouts. Reid happens to be out of the camp at the time, but takes cover nearby and watches the ensuing events. The Guardians make themselves comfortable and stage a drunken feast. Then they call for music and are enthralled by the tunes that Stobrod and Pangle produce. 'Good God, these is holy men,' says one Guardsman to the chief. 'Their mind turns on matters kept secret from the likes of you and me.' The chief then orders Stobrod and Pangle to stand in front of a nearby tree and has his men shoot them. Reid runs away to Ada's farm and tells Ada and Ruby what has transpired.

"Ada and Ruby assume from Reid's tale that both Stobrod and Pangle are dead. The women prepare to go to the shooting site, a substantial distance, for the purpose of burying the bodies. First Ruby gives Reid detailed instructions for getting back home to Georgia. Reid leaves, but we find later that he is something of a lazy mooch who never stays away from the farm for very long. The women set out in the snow, winter having arrived. Ada comments on the way that Reid doesn't seem like much of a man. Ruby says she finds him 'not particularly worse than the general order of men, which is to say that he would greatly benefit from having someone's foot in his back every waking minute.'

"The women find and bury Pangle's body but fail to locate Stobrod. Eventually Ada finds him, gravely wounded, under a rock ledge where he has managed to take cover. Ruby digs a bullet out of his back and administers other first aid based on her extensive knowledge of bush medicine. Stobrod needs to be taken to some kind of shelter, but Ruby says he wouldn't survive the trip back to the farm. She knows of another place, so they head out with Stobrod strapped to the back of their horse. The trek leads them to an abandoned Indian village with several huts still in good shape. This offers an occasion for much politically correct lamentation about the fate of the Indians and the Trail of Tears and so forth. At length the text lets the women make camp and settle into the process of nursing Stobrod back to health.

"The stories of Inman and Ada are soon to merge. Inman finally reaches Ada's farm and finds nobody there but Reid, who has drifted back rather than going to Georgia. From Reid he hears about the shooting of Stobrod and Pangle and the departure of the women to bury their bodies. He proceeds to the shooting site, based on Reid's directions, but finds only one grave and evidence that the women have stopped there. He follows their tracks into the wilderness and begins to lose his way as the tracks are obscured by new snowfall. He is practically delirious from hunger, having had no food for several days since the baby bear, but he makes a vow 'to eat nothing until he found Ada.' Other histrionics impinge. Then he hears a gunshot, which Ada has fired at a turkey, and he finds her in the woods. At the sight of her he is 'overcome by love like a ringing in his soul.' He's in such terrible shape that Ada doesn't recognize him for a while. But then she does and, brushing away a tear, leads him back to the Indian village. The reunion is on.

"Inman and Stobrod recuperate. When not in Inman's presence, Ruby tells Ada that 'we don't need him.' Ada replies, 'I know I don't need him, but I think

I want him.' There are escalating moments of intimacy between Ada and Inman, and signs of jealousy on Ruby's part. Various plans are made. Inman and Ada agree that Ruby will stay on at Ada's farm, and Ruby lays out her vision for its further development. Inman thinks about operating a portable sawmill that will keep him busy elsewhere. At Ada's instigation, she and Inman start having sex.

"Inman and Ada ponder his prospects for surviving the last months of the war. Rather than staying in the mountains and being hunted by the Home Guard, or rejoining the army and being thrown back into battle, he decides to travel north and place himself at the mercy of the Federals. The plan is to relocate their whole party from the Indian village to Ada's farm before Inman heads north. Inman and Stobrod are traveling well behind the two women and getting near the farm when they are attacked by five members of the Home Guard. Inman puts Stobrod out of danger by driving away the horse he is riding, then proceeds to shoot or bludgeon all but one Guardsman. This survivor is 'but a boy' whom Inman is reluctant to kill. A moment arrives when Inman has the drop on the boy but doesn't shoot, whereupon the boy fires and Inman goes down.

"Ada runs to the scene and finds Inman still alive. She holds him in her lap. He drifts in and out of consciousness and experiences 'a bright dream of a home,' which is described in glowing detail. The narrator's eye draws back to show a 'distant tableau' of 'a pair of lovers...

touching each other with great intimacy,' in a scene of 'such quiet and peace' that an optimistic observer would visualize 'long decades of happy union stretched before the two on the ground.' And that's it. We hear no more about the winter of 1864-65.

"Yet the book isn't quite done. It has a four-page epilogue—actually just three pages of text—dated October of 1874. The scene is Ada's farm on an idyllic late afternoon. We find both Stobrod and Reid still around. After employing Reid as a field hand, Ruby has married him and turned him into 'not a half-bad' man through a regime of hugs and kicks. ('A foot in the back when that was needed, a hug otherwise. It worked out to about equal measures.') Ruby has now given birth to three children, all boys. We also find that Ada has a daughter. She is nine years old, the right age to have sprung from Ada's liaison with Inman at the Indian village. But there is no mention of Inman, from which we conclude that he didn't survive his last encounter with the Home Guard."

"Do we really know he's not there?" asked Darnell.

"Yes, the author makes sure we know it by having the dinner table set with eight plates, just enough for the four children plus Ada, Ruby, Stobrod and Reid. The scene is one of complete domestic bliss, but Inman isn't part of it.

"The payoff of the book is delivered in the opening paragraph of the epilogue, before we get the abovementioned details. This reads as follows:

Even after all this time and three children together, Ada still found them clasping each other at the oddest moments. In the barn loft after knocking down the mud-cup nests of swallows. Behind the smokehouse after stoking a fire with wet cobs and hickory limbs. Earlier this day, it had been out in the potato field while breaking up the ground with big grubbing hoes. They had stood awkward and wide-footed in the furrows, each embracing with one arm, gripping the hoes with their free hands.

"There's a whole lot of embracing going on. Whom is Ada embracing? It's not Stobrod or Reid, so it must be Ruby. How much should we make of this? In one conspicuous word, the author tells us how much. Ada considers Ruby's three boys to be their children <u>together</u>. They are hers, meaning Ruby is hers. Hugs-and-kicks Reid has just been a sperm donor. Regardless of physical consummation or the lack thereof, what we've been reading isn't a heterosexual love story but a lesbian love story.

"Well, maybe this is an overstatement, since Ada could have gone either way. But that's the author's whole point. He puts same-sex love and heterosexual love on a par and suggests that any given woman may be capable of both. These soon became routine perspectives in the present century, but were still too radical for the mainstream in the 1990s. The author of *Cold Mountain* had to be feeling mighty slick about slipping them into a book that could sell three million copies and launch a major motion picture."

12

SUSTAINABILITY

"Well, looks like it's just you and me." Professor Bingham scanned the classroom again to verify that the only student present was Darnell. "As it happens, I told the university administration yesterday that I would be retiring at the end of this semester. Not a minute too soon, it seems.

"Under the circumstances I can take liberties with the rest of this course. Darnell, is there anything in particular you'd like me to talk about?"

"Dr. Bingham, if you don't mind my saying so, you've gotten a reputation on campus as a conservative, a contrarian opposed to social change. You're suspected of harboring theories in support of this position that go well beyond the material taught in your classes. I'd like to hear what these theories are. Maybe I can give you a critique."

"Okay, you're on. I do have what could be called a theory about gender relations, mainly revolving around male psychology, which has big implications for the long-term future. It doesn't tell how things will work out, but says that further trends will be shaped by factors nobody is considering today. The explanation may run over the class period, but I can lay it out if you like."

"Sure. Why not?"

"Before getting started, I should make two things clear. First, I'm not an advocate of fighting progress. What I always mean by 'progress' is the cultural evolution that involves the disestablishment of gender and the feminization of society. People sheltered by change-resistant institutions—usually meaning religions—can perhaps fight this kind of progress at little cost to themselves or others, but members of the general population will do more harm than good by going against the social grain. The progressive ascendency will eventually encounter opposition having nothing to do with public policy or collective action. The task on all sides will be to accommodate the resulting conflict rather than to hasten or modify it.

"Second, the progress at issue has only one downside—one legitimate basis for objection—which is almost never the target of conservative complaint. Social feminization undoubtedly has a cost for most males, and yields some changes in male and female postures that make women less satisfied with men, but there's no reason to assume that the net female benefit doesn't fully offset the male cost. Insofar as feminization involves relative dominance, there's no sense in arguing against it on the basis of fairness. Men ruled the world for scores of millennia, so it would be quite fair for women to hold sway for millennia going forward. And as indicated by the listing of male-associated and female-associated values in my lecture on political correctness, a feminized world promises to be a generally nicer place than the male-dominated sort.

"The one downside of progress is that a feminized culture is quite unlikely to be reproductively sustainable. Without some form of large-scale intervention it won't produce enough children to keep its population from declining. This is only one problem, but in the long run it's the mother of all problems. The presentation of my so-called theory will be mostly concerned with explaining why it exists. Then I may talk about possible demographic outcomes.

"So, Darnell, what's your definition of 'patriarchy'?"

"Male domination."

"Mine is a functional definition that works out basically the same. What I mean by patriarchy is any social system that lets men feel different from women. This is a basic need that I'll be talking about at some length. In theory men could feel different from women with none of the worldly privileges and almost none of the distinctions that have always been associated with patriarchy. For example, men could be assigned some religious role wherein they palavered together without bothering anybody else, while men and women led identical lives in all other respects. But since there's no record of such a system prevailing over time, we must associate patriarchy in practice with instances of male privilege. Domination is a broader condition than privilege, but we may as well assume its existence as well.

"Throughout nearly all of human history, patriarchy was universal. I'm using the term 'universal' in the not-quite-absolute sense traditionally employed by anthropologists. They applied it to the incest taboo, for example, while acknowledging isolated exceptions like the old obligation of Hawaiian fathers to deflower their daughters.

"When the war against patriarchy got underway in the last decades of the past century, there were myriad quasi-academic efforts to deny that patriarchy had been universal in the above sense. The simplest ploy consisted of representing matrilineal social structure—wherein members of a past culture traced their lineage through female ancestors, and a husband might have to join his wife's household or community—as a form of organization without male-favoring role divisions and areas of privilege. Cases of female gods and occasional female rulers and warriors were likewise cited as patriarchy-denying. The more elaborate efforts involved anthropological investigations, conducted in large part by members of university literature and gender studies departments, purporting to show that matriarchal or gender-balanced cultures had once been abundant.

Audiences were asked to believe that some mysterious force had caused all the given cultures to evaporate just before their acquisition of written language would have passed along firm evidence of their enlightened characteristics.

"In the present century these efforts were swept away by a new wave of opinion saying it didn't matter whether patriarchy had been universal or not. This didn't matter because the ongoing process of social feminization had become unstoppable and because academia had never been able to explain why patriarchy was once so prevalent. The matter was wrapped up with a scholarly verdict that, in effect, all of human history had been a mistake, a mere accident signifying nothing."

"Wait a minute," interjected Darnell. "Whether or not you're right in saying patriarchy had been universal, it existed simply because men could get away with it. Men were generally bigger and stronger than women, and testosterone made them more aggressive, and women were burdened by pregnancy and nursing and other requirements to perpetuate the species. So patriarchy was a natural condition until rising intelligence and technical advancement forced an approach toward gender equality."

"Good, you've hit the issue straight-on. The question is why patriarchy ever prevailed, and much of what we need to cover will emerge from showing that your answer is inadequate if not flatly wrong. The question can posed another way by asking whether patriarchy ever had a function. Before they gave up responding to significant questions altogether, the feminist pioneers stood solidly behind a premise that patriarchy could not have had a positive function, because if so its abolition might create some kind of cost. Nevertheless we can proceed by demonstrating that some positive function must have existed.

"There's no question that patriarchy had many costs. Other than relatively harmless features like male-only powwows, the hallmark of patriarchy was the existence of gender-based role divisions, which among other things let men look down on whatever tasks women did. Assigning human activities on the basis of gender was inherently expensive because gender had little to do with capability for pursuits not directly involving maternity or physical strength. Even in those areas there was a great deal of overlap. Despite the typical male edge in physical prowess, every society had many women better suited to be hunters and warriors than many men, especially with age and health taken into account. Yet the hunters and warriors were almost always male. Exceptions to this pattern were noted in song and story mainly because they were rare. Lack of female access to positions of leadership may have been less marked, but was even more damaging. Effective leadership was a matter of brainpower, and nearly all of it on the female side was wasted."

"I see where you're going with this," said Darnell. "You're going to say that if patriarchy had serious costs, it must have had some offsetting value. But I'm not ready to buy the costs. Take hunting and fighting. If you'll grant that proficiency in these activities required a lot of training from childhood onward, and that children at the appropriate starting age bore no sign of their future potential other than gender, it made perfect sense to focus training on the males and thereby establish the future role division. This gave the best odds of putting the right people into martial arts, while preserving females for the reproductive role that only they could play."

"Okay, there was indeed a substantial basis for traditional role divisions. But it doesn't explain the typical rigidity of those divisions, particularly the extent to which they wasted female brainpower. You could argue that when women had to average more than a half-dozen pregnancies just to sustain a population, they didn't have time for leadership. I would counter that a baby at the breast wouldn't be a barrier to decision-making, and that even women thus encumbered should have offered better leadership potential than men because they were more apt to keep their heads. You can say men were loath to accept female leadership, and I can say this was an effect rather than a cause of traditional role assignments. You can point to the male edge in spatial relations and the female capacity for nurturance as natural supports for hunting and childrearing respectively, and I can point out that these capacities were developed over the millennia precisely because gender roles evolved the way they did. We can debate these and other points ad infinitum, but I don't think you can get around the fact that gender-based role assignments went beyond anything necessary or rational, meaning they had a cost.

"Also please keep in mind that patriarchy didn't just prevail among primordial hunter-gatherers. It stayed alive and well right up through the industrial age. At the start of the twentieth century the world's commitment to patriarchy was still so strong and unquestioned that it caused Sigmund Freud, the trail-blazing explorer of the human psyche, to get some things completely backward. At any rate I'll take it as given, even if you're not ready to agree, that in most if not all contexts patriarchy had a cost—economic or martial or both. The question then is why it remained so pervasive.

"Competition was nature's way of allocating scarce resources, and groups of human beings had to compete not only with other animals but also with each other. Inter-group contact inevitably brought competition among different forms of social organization. Those that yielded the greatest competitive advantages should have prevailed as evolutionary outcomes. Over the course of history all imaginable forms of organization were surely tested for at least short periods. There had to have been patriarchal societies and matriarchal societies and intermediate cases. Sometimes gender ruled and sometimes it carried little weight. So humanity had ample opportunities to find and embrace optimal arrangements. These should have tended toward gender-neutral meritocracy—yet patriarchy kept winning out.

"When faced with something puzzling about an animal or its behavior, evolutionary biologists have always told each other to 'look first to reproduction.' The quoted rationale is that, in descending order of importance, 'there is reproduction, and there is everything else.' Politically cowered academics have always resisted applying this lesson to their own species. Yet the circumstances clearly suggest that patriarchy was a reproductive strategy. That's what it was for. It dominated human societies despite its costs because it was instrumental in getting them from one generation to the next. Nothing else can account for it.

"Patriarchy shouldn't have been necessary just to obtain enough babies, given the easy terms of their creation and the fact that nature had made the human female the sexiest creature on the planet. Reproductive strategies could have deployed seduction or orgies or even rape without the expense of establishing other social arrangements on a sexist basis. One of the more plausible ideas has been that patriarchy was an outgrowth of monogamy and polygamy, advancing the development of complex social organization by letting males focus on their own biological offspring. But female sexual exclusiveness could have been supported without all the other patriarchal baggage typically observed, and patriarchy prevailed in contexts where such exclusiveness did not. There had to be a further explanation.

"Men can't have babies. This is the only thing I'll be saying from now on that isn't speculative, but it goes a long way. Launching a new life is the most important thing anyone can do, and men can't do it. In assessing the impact of mothering it's impossible to separate the act of childbearing from the mutually instinctive attachment that follows. Some men can partially replicate the latter component but not the whole package, and in any case they've rarely been asked to try. So across the millennia of human development, life began with an extended interval in which Mom was the world.

"Sigmund Freud misinterpreted a lot of what he saw, but he knew where to look, and where he looked for explanations of human personality and behavior was early childhood. There he came upon the origins of what I'll be calling the gender dilemma. Due to patriarchal bias he got the paradigm backward, identifying something as 'penis envy' that actually derived from existential issues and didn't involve the child's gender. What really happened on the gender front was the acquisition by males of a chronic inferiority complex. Nothing they experienced later would ever equal the power of Mom. This made them spend the rest of their days trying to compensate for the fact that they weren't women. Their compensatory mechanism was patriarchy."

"I'm having trouble with your implication that a woman's capacity for childbirth is a great gift that justifies some offsetting amount of male oppression. How can the need to carry an infant around for nine months be construed as anything besides a burden? And what's the justification for assuming that women have some kind of post-natal advantage? Today we're taught that as participants in childrearing, men can function precisely the same as women from the moment of birth onward."

"They can, but they don't. Actually most of them can't. Women spent hundreds of thousands of years learning how to be proper mothers, and if we depended on a majority of men to catch up with them the species would go extinct long before this happened. Some men can make fine mommies, just as some can high-jump six feet or solve differential equations, but most can't. Or more to the point, most won't, which is essentially the same thing for reasons I'll be discussing.

"As for your calling pregnancy a burden, I'm not saying it isn't. I'm saying the female capacity for childbirth and what comes afterward is a source of grounding and identity that males not only lack but spend their lives trying to replicate. The magic of motherhood may even bear some positive linkage to the intrusiveness of pregnancy and the time it requires. And a woman who doesn't want to endure the burden can avoid having children and still get a great deal of the gain. It's built into her as a human female.

"The modern era has brought a view that the patriarchal urge was a product of intellectual backwardness and thus should dissipate as people got smarter. This view aligned with cultural trends for a while, but as an historical generalization it was exactly wrong. From the beginning of human development through recent millennia, the male need for compensation was steadily intensified by gains in self-awareness and juvenile dependence and maternal importance. A chimpanzee or bonobo didn't have time or resources or inclination to draw life-meanings from his birth and initial nurturance, whereas humans increasingly did. Intelligence wasn't the solution; it was the problem.

"One can easily see how men managed to impose patriarchal systems on women. Patriarchy ruled because women allowed it, and women allowed it because circumstances gave them no choice. The situation was essentially a deal, though it wasn't reached by any sort of conscious negotiation. The physical vulnerability of the human species meant females couldn't survive without a full complement of males. While possible in concept, communities that limited their male presence by some combination of infanticide and male banishment would have been very difficult to maintain and support and defend. In practice the sexes had to live and work together, and patriarchal systems became necessary because such arrangements were the only terms on which males would fully do their part.

"There may have been continuity between these arrangements and primordial mammalian traditions of alpha males and harems and so forth. Maybe testosterone and dimorphism were involved. But such possibilities aren't a necessary part of the explanation and thus don't merit speculation. The essential foundation of patriarchy as it entered recorded history was psychological, not biological. The driver was the male compensatory imperative, a byproduct of evolving intelligence, and the facilitator was an accrued female awareness that patriarchy was the price of male support.

"Men have always needed to feel different from women. In concept they may not have needed to feel better than women, or to give themselves greater overall importance. I've mentioned a harmless role division that could possibly have satisfied them. But in practice, because compensatory behavior was never fully convincing, compensation meant overcompensation. So males went on to dominate most decision-making and to restrict gender roles in ways that let them view women as subordinate. Margaret Meade, one of the best anthropologists writing before academia got politicized, once noted that, 'no matter what men do, they always consider it more important than what women do.' Because of other concerns she never asked why, and this question was soon lost in a cloud of male indictment.

"Little or none of the male compensatory need arose from contact with adult females. It came from childhood, when the power of Mom was infinite, and consequently it had no limit or threshold of satisfaction. The levels of patriarchy prevailing across history weren't outcomes based on fairness or relative happiness, but ecological solutions that traded off the functional benefits of making males feel good about themselves against the functional costs thereby incurred.

"The male problem went beyond ego gratification. The challenge faced by the barren gender was one of self-definition. Women always knew who they were. The lowliest mother was individualized by the uniqueness of her children and by her unique importance to them. The capacity for childbirth created a female identity that underlay other aspects of personhood and largely existed, as I've said, whether the capacity was exercised or not. But male identity had to be built from scratch. This was the job of the male cult."

"Enough. You seem to have quite a construct, and apparently there's more, but it's time to start objecting. You're basically saying that all male behavior is compensatory. Or most of it, or key elements of it. But I haven't seen or felt anything to support that. I'm not compensating for anything. I feel no need to look down upon or distinguish myself from other people, male or female, and there's little sign that the men around me do either. Beg pardon, but I think you're imagining the whole thing."

"Indeed, there's a problem of perspective in your case. It involves your position in the world, and the availability of substitutes for gender heroism, and the fact that the traditional male-making machinery was barely visible by the time you arrived. I'll need to hold the explanation until we've gotten further along, if you don't mind waiting.

"Kindly go back to thinking about past centuries and consider what you know from literature and coursework and general exposure. Human history was in large part a story of male displays and posturing and acting-out and egregious self-aggrandizement. Nothing could account for all this besides the male compensatory syndrome. It was as plain as the nose on your face.

"To review, we've shown that patriarchy must have had a positive function to offset its costs, and we've identified this function as allowing men to feel different from women. We've talked about the power of motherhood, the psychological basis of patriarchy, the problem of intelligence, the male compensatory imperative, and the male challenge of self-definition. This has brought us to the support system that I call the male cult. Again I'll proceed in the past tense since the cult is no longer what it was.

"The male cult was a shadowy functionality that operated as a definitional system and a hero generator and a club. Its only fixed rules were that no girls were allowed and no female influence was tolerated. Men would almost never let women define them. The main characteristics of the cult as a club were that all males in early youth wanted to join; that a great majority did join by the time they were adults; and that membership once acquired could never be renounced, regardless of intentions or perceptions to the contrary.

"The male cult was everywhere. Perhaps it should be described in plural terms as a multiplicity of cults that pursued the same objective in different ways. On these terms there would be an umbrella cult serving each nation or major social grouping, with sub-cults addressing various components of the population. Such a description would allow for the fact that the gatekeepers of manhood often worked at cross-purposes and even came into open conflict, especially when their male images were linked to ethnicity or social class. But given the cult's fluidity and evanescence, any attempt to compartmentalize it would quickly get lost in complications. So one can best envision the cult as a single vast network of agents operating in myriad and ever-changing collaborations.

"The tasks of the male cult consisted of identifying the personal characteristics and behaviors associated with manliness; endowing these characteristics with heroic stature; limiting female access to such heroism; and validating cult membership for applicants found worthy to share in the manly estate. The first three tasks were almost always executed on a collaborative basis, generally at a cultural or sub-cultural level, whereas validation could be effected by any instrumentality at any level.

"The definitional task typically started with physiological attributes such as those favoring males as hunters and warriors. Men claimed ownership of activities and behaviors that involved power and use of force, while characteristics involving nurturance were assigned to females by virtue of maternity. Erection of a patriarchal system then led to elaboration of these polarities. As enforcers of the system, males came to stand for hierarchy and all things executive, while females were left with communality, love, peace, forgiveness and so forth. Progress brought further associations such as logic with males and intuition with females. All these polarities were mentioned in my talk on political correctness. The details didn't really matter, however, because the characteristics chosen to define manhood had little bearing on the cult's mission. Men might just as well have gone for intuition and left logic to women.

"What counted was maintaining the chosen associations and the heroism accruing to the male side of each. Ideally this meant preventing females from exhibiting the male-claimed characteristics, using whatever mechanisms were available and affordable in the given context. The fallback was denial that such characteristics existed when females displayed them, or denial that they could have heroic stature in female hands. A patriarchal system at peak form could find male affirmation in deeds that females performed in exactly the same way. For a woman, supporting a family was mere necessity, whereas for a man it was the heroic job of bringing home the bacon. A woman couldn't be brave even when she was brave, because only men—and by extension all validated men—were allowed to possess the heroic attribute of bravery.

"The cult's validation task was accomplished most efficiently via formal induction rituals like lion hunts, trials by ordeal, bar mitzvahs and so forth. It tended to be a group effort but could be carried off by a single agent such as a father who happened to have the requisite male credibility. One of the gifts brought by validation was a capacity for self-imagining. A cult applicant might learn to share in the heroism accruing to male attributes and behaviors without actually exhibiting any of them, so long as his validators were also self-imaginers. A paradoxical aspect of the validation process was that it required constant renewal—which we can call affirmation—throughout life. Membership in the club could never be revoked, but due to the inherent shakiness of the male construct it never felt secure. Renewal was most often accomplished by reaching out to acknowledge the club membership of others. Affirmation was a reciprocal act, conferring the same benefits on the affirming agent as the affirmed.

"In this and all other respects, the process of male definition was circular and self-referential. Men were important because they were men, who were important. This sounds silly because it was. Manhood was always comical, the more so because it was taken so seriously. Any comments?"

"I have no way to judge any of this. Maybe I can grant you two things. One is that, while the male antics you've described seem terribly far-fetched, past patterns of male behavior were at least somewhat peculiar in ways consistent with your account. The other is that a lot of today's males could probably benefit from a collaborative support group like your cult. But these concessions stop way short of granting that elaborate male self-inflation and the resultant burdens placed upon women were positive for a society as a whole. How in the world were they justifiable?"

"They were justifiable because they helped—allowed—cultures to survive. To temper my rather bald description I should mention that, at least in more advanced societies, men almost never thought about or even noticed what they doing. They had no conscious awareness of belonging to any gender-related club. This held because the male cult was amorphous, because a lot of its operations were subtle, and because everyone thought making a fuss over manhood was perfectly natural. Men were, after all, important. The compensatory system bred and entailed a general blindness to the fact that women didn't celebrate themselves the same way because they didn't need to.

"I've referred to the cult as a creator of male heroism. The identity it offered in compensation for the psychologically one-down status of the barren gender was a heroic identity, widely variable but always pointedly male. The compensatory mission involved two distinct phases. The first covered early life from the initial awareness of gender through what I've called the validation process. The heroism acquired during this phase had to support a specifically male self-conception. But the same didn't hold for the maintenance doses of heroism required later. In adulthood various types of heroism became substitutable. Almost anything individualizing about a man's life could provide an adequate measure of heroic sustenance. The keys to an individualizing existence in more advanced societies were education and wealth and public exposure. These factors, or the lives they permitted, could relieve males of a need to see themselves or the world in gendered terms. In the present century this circumstance has become important to the process of dismantling patriarchy as I'll discuss later.

"Putting male heroism in proper perspective will require a substantial digression to establish a broader framework. In general, heroism can be any act or condition or award that makes its owner feel special. The most prominent form of heroism has always been what can be summarized as existential heroism. This was more prominent than gender heroism because the need for it extended to females as well as males, because its absence was felt more acutely, and because it had a more immediate bearing on a population's welfare. Either a failure or an excessive pursuit of existential heroism could kill off a society very fast, whereas a failure of male heroism promised only gradual demise.

"My survey of the psychological and sociological literature has shown a remarkable lack of attention to the male compensatory problem and its heroic solution. The gender dilemma has always been something that nobody wants to think about. But in the last century there did emerge a modest literature on the origins and nature of existential heroism. This came from what was called an 'existential synthesis' of reinterpreted Freudian concepts.

"Sigmund Freud's theories of instinct and infantile sexuality yielded some odd conclusions that included the development of a 'castration complex' among male children and 'penis envy' among girls. The existential synthesis replaced these overtly patriarchal views by asserting that the basic problem wasn't sex or even gender but mortality. Death wasn't fully understandable to children, but the related mind-body duality was an immediate concern. The child's otherwise unbounded self was found to be housed in a vulnerable shell with overtones of decay. The difficulty presented by the mother was her corporeality, her association with 'body-meanings' that were intrinsic to her motherhood and exuded determinism. Her symbolic burden of vulnerability caused children of both sexes to see dependence on her as a threat. They were attracted by the father's austere suggestion of immortality and thus turned toward him for reasons of difference from the mother. The male child focused on genitalia because they provided a basis of differentiation from her, not a source of sexual desire or castration anxiety.

"I won't dwell upon what happened in childhood according to the existential synthesis, which involved an 'Oedipal project' for both sexes rather than Freud's male-side 'Oedipal complex.' The important part was the lifetime acquisition of a 'primal guilt' based on horror of one's own animal condition, which as a child one couldn't understand and as an adult one couldn't accept.

"The adult solutions revolved around heroism of the sort I'm calling existential heroism. Ernest Becker, the leading writer on the subject, considered this heroism a 'reflex of the terror of death' and used the term to reference all actions and constructs designed to yield a sense of immortality. The desired sense was 'a feeling of primary value, of cosmic specialness, of ultimate usefulness to creation, of unshakeable meaning.' The pursuit of this heroism could be solitary, in the so-called artistic solution, but far more often was a collective enterprise. Becker said a society's customs, rules, statuses and roles were all designed to make it 'a vehicle for earthly hero-ism.' Society itself was a codified hero system, a 'living myth of the significance of human life,' making it a religion whether it thought so or not.

"The pursuit of existential heroism on an inter-personal basis was linked to the phenomenon of transference. This was a form of fetishism wherein a person projected certain attributes—which could be characteristics one wanted to possess or attributes having some relationship to one's worries and fears—onto a 'transference object' credited with reassuring powers. Usually the transference object was a leader or author-itative group that could make sense of life, or even mediate with the forces of the universe, while favor-ing the supplicant with conditional or unconditional approval. Transference could provide a so-called 'safe heroism' wherein the 'truth of the other' to which one surrendered was an uplifting and purportedly achiev-able template for behavior, and the 'other' serving as the transference object was accessible to provide ongoing heroic affirmation.

"How are we doing? I've kept speaking in the past tense since we'll be getting back to gender heroism, but pursuit of the existential variety is still robust and should be visible in your daily life."

"It's all rather interesting. In fact, based on my experience I can sort of buy existential heroism. But let's return to your male comedy."

"I've posited the existence of male heroism, or gen-der heroism, as a specifically male variety driven by a specifically male deficiency. Its parallels and areas of overlap with existential heroism shouldn't be overstated since the two types of heroics sought basically different kinds of compensation. Nevertheless they had three general connections. First, transference played a primary role in both cases. Second, both phenomena had origins in childhood exposure to maternal power. And third, males often relied upon compensatory heroics to augment existential heroism, because attainment of the existential variety was harder for males than for females.

"The male cult was a transference object of a special kind. The leader-follower relationship typical of transference was most prevalent among young males seeking validation. Thereafter, cult members tended to be both leaders and followers, bestowing as well as receiving maintenance doses of compensatory heroism. The cult continued to serve as a transference object, but in a shadowy fashion, and the same held for the ways in which it developed and sustained a heroic definition of maleness.

"Existential heroism and gender heroism bore different linkages to maternal power. According to the existential synthesis, the strength of a mother's role worked together with her aura of mortality to create a threat that her child tried to escape, and the child's withdrawal was a first step in renouncing attempts at self-creation to rely instead on socially conferred heroism. Maternal impact was just one part of the developmental scenario that led to adult reliance on existential heroism, whereas it was the root cause of male compensatory heroics.

"Given that developers of the existential synthesis paid little attention to gender-specific outcomes, I've looked around in the literature of the relevant period to see if anybody else made the connection. It turned out that a few feminist writers did, but they only pursued the subject to a limited extent dictated by their mission. These writers, who included some professional psychotherapists, revisited early childhood development in search of explanations for the dominance-submission syndrome and sadomasochism. Drawing on various kinds of evidence, they joined with the existential theorists in burying the Freudian concept of the mother figure as a weakling. Children instead saw the mother as an extremely powerful figure. This was a major reason why both boys and girls needed to escape from dependence on her. For males the escape became a process of "defensive differentiation," which led to the subsequent male penchant for dominance and sadism. But this syndrome was as far as the given writers went, because their objective was denigration of males rather than reaching a broad understanding of the male compensatory imperative.

"Establishing a unified theory would require answering the question of why boys engaged in 'defensive differentiation' while girls did not. On one hand, the answer might just be that this pattern was forestalled for girls by their anatomical similarity to their mothers. On the other hand, since the defensive differentiation process carried forward to produce life-time consequences for males, the key factor might be their realization that they would never exercise the ultimate power. The first of these possibilities would leave the male compensatory need without any basis in developmental psychology and wouldn't seem to jibe with the existential synthesis. In rejecting Freud's scenario, the existential theorists attributed to boys and girls the same stages of early development, yielding a 'castration complex' in both cases. Defensive differentiation wouldn't put the sexes on separate pathways until a later time when children had abandoned bodily solutions to existential problems. So the decisive influence wouldn't be anatomical comparison per se but receipt of the message that little girls would grow up to be like their mothers whereas little boys would not. A patriarchal view would see this realization as constraining upon girls, but the burdensome nature of defensive differentiation would suggest that males were the constrained parties—that the message put little boys one-down and little girls one-up. In any case I'm not qualified to resolve this question, and scholars in the present century have lacked interest in understanding or even acknowledging the gender dilemma.

"The third connection between male compensatory behavior and existential heroism wasn't anything I've gathered from the literature. It involved the fact that male and female requirements for socially conferred heroism tended to differ because motherhood was naturally heroic. Motherhood automatically generated some of the specialness associated with existential heroism, since every child was unique and every mother was irreplaceable to her child. Even the act of giving life, at a cost of 'pain and sorrow,' was heroic. In the language of existential theorists, motherhood produced an interval of conjunction between animal and symbolic identities that men could never share. Consequently women required less transference-based heroism than men, or at least could obtain it more readily. The greater male need often led men to seek existential and gender heroism on a joint basis. Their life-justification drew on their cult-validated manliness and vice versa. Many cultures and some gender-laden religions were clearly structured to give men this sort of existential leg-up, although the connection became less common in advanced societies.

"My theoretical framework has another component relating to future demographic trends. I'll get into that after we've covered some highlights of the war against patriarchy, then will close with a look at possible long-run outcomes.

"Patriarchy lasted without serious challenge through the middle of the last century. What prevailed in advanced countries at mid-century would have to be described as soft patriarchy. Rigid barriers to female self-expression and economic independence had been overthrown, but there were still role divisions that gave males comfortable levels of gender-based identity and importance. Fear of unwanted pregnancy was still important in motivating women to accept traditional marriage and the strictures associated with male leadership.

"As emphasized in my lecture on political correctness, what changed everything was the arrival of safe, effective, female-deployable and male-undetectable birth control. Female emancipation had long been advancing on many fronts, but birth control of this nature was the catalyst that took the U.S. and other rich countries across a threshold at which the retreat of patriarchy became unstoppable. The initial impacts were largely limited to household disruption and rising female participation in the labor force. The 'women's movement' campaigned against limited aspects of patriarchy with mixed success. Then late in the century came political correctness, which attacked the entire patriarchal regime by denigrating every aspect of traditional maleness. Male compensatory heroism and the identity-creating operation of the male cult could not have been targeted more effectively if the activists had known exactly what they were doing.

"Moving into the present century, political correctness became less of a linguistic exercise and more of an implicit guideline for action. Its advance was led by the educational system, starting at the university level and working downward. Reflections of political correctness in government policy were slower to arrive and highly variable by region. Race played a significant role in the assault on traditional maleness, in part because calling people racist remained the most effective form of personal indictment.

"Impacts on male behavior and outlook began to be noticeable early in the century. By all sorts of indicators men were being gradually destabilized. Some became more apologetic, others became more defensive or defiant, and there was a general decline in male willingness to enter and maintain committed relationships with women. The U.S. fertility rate started to fall in the century's second decade and has been edging lower ever since. Male avoidance of commitment has probably shared responsibility for this pattern with economic factors and a general loss of female tolerance for men.

"Darnell, you had two questions earlier that I wasn't prepared to address at the time. One came during my lecture on political correctness and consisted of asking why so many men embraced what was essentially an anti-male posture. The other consisted of wondering why you don't personally feel any need for compensatory behavior of the type I've discussed."

"Right."

"The answer in both cases involves the substitutability of other forms of compensation for male-pattern gender heroism. Referring to my earlier comments about male validation and affirmation, the male cult has remained somewhat functional in its role of validating young people as cult members. Therefore you are probably a validated male like most of your predecessors in this century. Where alternative heroism comes into play is fulfillment of the male compensatory need that continues throughout life. It happens that as a student in a top-flight university, you're a member of an elite. This status relieves you of any need to denigrate women or exalt masculine virtues because it lets you look down on most people your age, both male and female. Your personal identity doesn't hinge on a sense of manhood requiring periodic affirmation. You don't have any conscious awareness of indulging in compensatory behavior, yet self-serving comparisons are at work."

"Well…maybe."

"Most of the males who embraced political correctness in its heyday were in similar positions. Whether or not they had elite status based on education or wealth or power, they led individualizing lives in some respect that let them dispense with gender heroism. When persuaded by arguments of fairness, these men often became active participants in the campaign against traditional maleness, with convenient gains from pleasing their female associates. They exerted a great deal of influence because by definition they included all males with power to command public attention.

"Many of these men found compensation in their minority status. So long as traditional views prevailed among his contemporaries, a male could acquire a sort of heroism by rejecting their values to place himself on higher moral ground. The product could be called counterheroism. It occasioned my comment earlier that membership in the male cult once acquired could never be renounced. The counterheroic male not only took pride in rejecting his masculine heritage but often considered this as evidence of psychological as well as moral superiority. He could side with female interests because his masculinity was *especially* secure. But in fact he was no less dependent than his contemporaries on pre-adult gifts from the cult he came to disparage.

"Personal counterheroism was a leading type of 'minority solution' to the gender dilemma, but it wasn't the only type. Minority solutions could exist at any scale that let one group look down upon a larger and more traditional group. For example, the whole country of Sweden has functioned for a long time as a minority solution, deriving collective heroism from feeling superior to the world's gender-bound populations. This has probably done as much as surrogate fatherhood by the state to buck up Swedish birth rates. But minority solutions are bound to lose efficacy as minorities become majorities and the male cult loses its residual power to validate new members. In the long run the gender dilemma has no solution.

"Now let's start looking ahead. Within the remainder of this century you will start to see the dismantling of a second mechanism whereby patriarchy supported reproductive success. This second reproductive assist involved female psychology rather than male psychology and will take a minute to explain.

"Feminists at the end of the last century liked to insist that all gender differences were culturally determined, while never asking why cultures throughout history had found it necessary to do so much determining. In the writings of that period I only found one passage touching upon this necessity. It came in a book called *Dark Sun* by Julia Kristeva, a French-Bulgarian psychoanalyst and linguist, and ran as follows (with a paraphrase in the middle for brevity):

> *One cannot overemphasize the tremendous psychic, intel-*
> *lectual, and affective effort a woman must make in order*
> *to find the other sex as erotic object. [When combined*
> *with the translation of physical self-discovery into symbolic*
> *terms,] shifting…to a sexual object of a sex other than*
> *that of the primary maternal object represents a gigantic*
> *elaboration in which a woman cathexes a psychic potential*
> *greater than what is demanded of the male sex.*

"Why exactly did the survival of the human species come to depend on a 'tremendous effort' involving 'gigantic elaboration,' and what mechanism assured that all this cathexing would take place?

"Actually there are three questions, of which the first is why instinct didn't do the whole job of erotically fixating females on males. Its answer is that much of the payoff from rising human intelligence came in the form of greater flexibility. Instinct was antithetical to flexibility, so reliance on instinct had to decline in most areas of life. The hard-wired components of sexuality remained important, but couldn't be entrusted with the whole mating process in a species as complicated as we became.

"The second question is why the gap between instinctive and socially desired behavior required so much psychic effort for females to cross. The reason for this was Mom. Human advancement and rising intelligence were largely female products because they entailed and fed upon progressively longer maternal dependence and richer bonding of mothers and children. The outcome in each case was an emotional-cum-erotic attachment to a female object. For girls the attachment, or the energy behind it, had to be redirected toward males as a reproductive necessity. This developmental task may have been trivial early on, but as we got smarter it became more and more challenging. As was true for the male compensatory imperative, intelligence wasn't the solution; it was the problem.

"The third question—how the redirection was brought about—is easiest because it has only one possible answer. Society had to pick up where instinct left off, so the redirective mechanism had to be societal, meaning culturally imposed. The people in charge of cultural imposition in general and male glorification in particular were men themselves. The patriarchal apparatus that drove and orchestrated male self-imagining existed to attract and preempt female erotic attention as well as to render the male condition tolerable. By their own account, men possessed unique value as sexual objects because they were so terribly impressive and important. Girls bought into this message before they were old enough to know better, and thereafter were mostly kept in its thrall by constant repetition.

"Feminists once spoke of a feminine mystique, but this construct was just a focus for complaint. The operative mystique was male. It was the masculine ideal, the malehead, the composite of all the dreams and projections and exaltations sponsored by the male cult. It was the image the cult put forth for women to adore. Though women in traditional societies spent a lot of energy competing for men, what really mattered was making men worthy of such attention. Economic power and the other tangible attractions that men gave themselves went a long way in this regard, but the male mystique provided an essential foundation.

"So what's bound to happen as the male cult is fully dismantled and men lose their modes of self-creation is that women will lose their overriding sexual orientation toward men. The male mystique may take a long time to go away—like the grin of the Cheshire cat it may outlast its visible supports—but eventually it will disappear. At that point typical women will feel no more sexual attraction toward men than toward other women. In fact, thanks to Mom, they may tend to feel less.

"This process is already underway. As of midcentury in the U.S., more than a quarter of all sexual contacts involving females consist of liaisons between women. This share will continue to rise until it is well over half. Even if the typical woman becomes indifferent between having sex with men and women, rather than favoring the latter, long-term sexual relationships will become heavily weighted toward pairs of women because men will be relatively unattractive as partners. Destabilization of males due to loss of cult support and opportunities for compensatory behavior will make them increasingly averse to commitment and difficult to manage. So within a century or two the standard reproductive household will consist of two women and one or two children.

"In concept, males could pair up with each other and raise children at a rate similar to that of female-only households. But this won't happen for three reasons. First, although they will increasingly seek sexual recourse with each other, men collectively will never lose their primary sexual orientation toward women. Second, within the foreseeable future most men won't acquire either the talent or the proclivity to take the lead in traditionally female roles. And third, there won't be a source for the huge number of babies that male-only households would have to acquire to put them on a reproductive par with female-only households.

"The reproductive problem of single-sex pairing amounts to a misallocation of resources. Men offer a great deal less support for children when women are absent than when they are present. The difference is a waste of parenting resources. Patriarchy, with all its costs, achieved a workable allocation of resources by letting men feel good about themselves and getting women to accept them. As I've said, it was a reproductive strategy. There's no other reproductive strategy of similar effectiveness in sight.

"It's worthwhile or at least entertaining to consider the possible long-run outcomes of our reproductive problem..."

"We're now getting into wild guesses, right?"

"Well, you could call my whole theory a wild guess, although I think its main features are blindingly obvious. At any rate we are indeed entering an area of pure speculation. There are some logical limits, but not many.

"What I'll do is lay out a series of cases, or scenarios. For completeness I'll include a couple that contradict statements already made. The single requirement is that a scenario must involve a constant population, meaning a demographic equilibrium in which births plus perhaps net immigrants equal deaths. It doesn't matter how far the population may decline before the equilibrium is reached, so long as it doesn't fall so low that the country will inevitably be overrun by another culture. Many of the cases I'll be presenting aren't mutually exclusive, so keep in mind that equilibrium may be attained most easily via a combination of scenarios. Also, I'm assuming away perpetual increases in longevity. Obviously a demographic equilibrium will be more imaginable if the human lifespan is expected to keep rising without limit.

"The initial scenarios will pertain just to the U.S., although they will apply similarly to other advanced countries. The first is that women come to understand the gender dilemma and accept the male compensatory imperative. On this basis women allow the continuation of a very soft form of patriarchy in which males retain some latitude for cult-supported self-creation. Heterosexual pairing continues to predominate, and improvements in male behavior allow the nation's fertility rate to recover. But the probability of this scenario is zero. Women—especially those at the top of the educational scale—will never accept the premise that men are inherently one-down in the gender balance. They will continue to set aside the power of motherhood and insist on equalizing everything else. Although France sometimes looks like an exception, the whole advanced world seems to be going this way.

"The second scenario is the feminist ideal. In response to centuries of relentless pressure, men finally stop trying to feel different from women. As parents they become identical with women from the moment of birth onward. This allows motherhood to disappear as anything other than a momentary biological accident. Heterosexual mating declines due to female indifference between male and female partners, but new-model males are so willing and able to parent on their own that the fertility rate holds up. The probability of this scenario is also zero. Most men will never accept being women-without-wombs, and motherhood will never die until we do.

"The third scenario may appear far-fetched but is among the more plausible as a partial reproductive solution. The problem with males, over and above the gender dilemma, is that they are reproductive dead weight. Women must supply all the babies. When males and females are roughly equal in number, the population-sustaining fertility rate—the so-called replacement rate—is slightly over two children per woman. But if females outnumber males, the replacement rate goes down. For example, if the ratio is two-to-one, the replacement rate declines by one-quarter to a bit over 1.5. Down goes the female burden of achieving demographic stability.

"Some evidence of this scenario already exists. The ongoing destabilization of males due to loss of cult support has rendered male children increasingly troublesome to raise. Hence some women are selecting for female offspring. Under natural conditions male children slightly outnumber females, but this margin has already been reversed in the U.S. A much greater tendency to select for females can be expected as male behavior continues to deteriorate and new technology allows the selection process to occur *in vitro* rather than via abortion. This tendency in itself isn't likely to reduce the replacement fertility rate far enough to stabilize the population, given the expected decline in actual fertility, but it could contribute substantially to a demographic equilibrium.

"The two other scenarios for the U.S. involve immigration. This factor has prevented any decline in the nation's population through midcentury—due in part to the relative fecundity of immigrants after their arrival—and is bound to be an important stabilizing factor in the future. For expository purposes I'm drawing a hazy distinction between immigration scenarios based on the types of people who arrive. I'll be using the term 'left' to denote people with progressive social values and 'right' to denote those with traditionalist, patriarchal values. It can be assumed that the right always outbreeds the left, while political recruitment in a progressive environment always draws people from right to left.

"The favorable immigration scenario is one in which the arriving population is either left or susceptible to leftward recruitment. This has been largely the case in the U.S. up to now. Our arrivals have come very largely from Latin American and Asian countries where traditional values may still prevail but are not vociferously defended as parts of the culture. After one to three generations such persons blend into the existing population without a great deal of political conflict. Their fertility rates decline toward the non-population-sustaining levels exhibited by other groups, so further immigration is required on an ongoing and perhaps escalating basis to maintain a demographic equilibrium.

"The unfavorable scenario is one in which immigrants are increasingly hard-right in social orientation. These persons bring cultures that are strongly resistant to change, usually because their traditions are anchored in religious doctrine. They assimilate slowly if at all and are accompanied by political conflict, ghettoization and attendant problems. An upside is that their fertility rates remain high enough to moderate the required immigration flows. Nevertheless their number may reach a point at which it threatens the progressive social order.

"Now I'll mention three alternative cases for the world as a whole, which in the long run will have an important bearing on what happens in the U.S.

"The first scenario is one in which the entire world goes left. Progressive values win out everywhere, presumably accompanied by a movement toward economic and technological equality among regions. In this case migrants to the U.S. will create no disharmony—if the nation can retain some basis for attracting them. But since the gender dilemma knows no political boundaries, the world's fertility rate will fall below replacement level and the global population will begin to decline. The question is whether anything will eventually happen to stabilize the population at some lower level. Perhaps when the human species is sufficiently thin on the ground, some kind of frontier mentality will take hold as a source of reproductive inspiration. Or perhaps the global population will simply fall asymptotically to zero."

"Oh, come on. It's ridiculous to think that the species might let itself go extinct for no reason other than reproductive lethargy."

"I don't consider this first global scenario very likely, but it's not impossible. Keep in mind that never in human history has the gender dilemma been allowed to play out. Never has there been any demographic influence like birth control. Well, you could say that the coming of agriculture was an equally momentous influence in a positive direction. But population gains always run into natural limits of some sort, whereas declines due to reproductive failure have no limit other than zero. Anyway, who would have guessed a century ago that even with immigration, the collective population of the rich world would be declining by now?

"The second global scenario is one in which the world's cultures remain divided between left and right, progressive and traditional. A likely feature of this case is that the traditional societies remain economically and technologically underdeveloped, because the religious strictures required to keep the relevant traditions in place are antithetical to progress across the board. Another likely feature is antipathy toward the left by societies on the right, due to a combination of fear and envy and awareness that the left is reproductively parasitic on the right. The uneasy situation that results might resemble the faceoff between communism and capitalism during the Cold War. The U.S. would probably be thrown into its latter immigration scenario, wherein a large share of immigrants are recruited from the hard right.

"In the third global case, the whole world goes right. Countries on the left are unable to draw population-sustaining numbers of immigrants and accomplish their right-to-left recruitment fast enough to maintain a progressive hegemony. Or possibly there is use of force, which the targeted societies are too politically correct to resist. In either case, patriarchy returns under cover of religion. Theocracy prevails. Civilization grinds to a halt.

"Okay, okay, I won't go any further. Who knows what will actually happen? Maybe we will learn to live forever, making childbirth unnecessary. I'm just trying to point out that we're in uncharted waters. There are epochal changes in store. As the evolutionary biologists used to say: "There is reproduction, and there is everything else.""